P·R·A·C·T·I·C·A·L
PARENTING
COOKING FOR KIDS

PRACTICAL PARENTING
P·R·A·C·T·I·C·A·L

COOKING FOR KIDS

SARA LEWIS

NOTES:

1. Standard level spoon measurements are used in all recipes.
1 tablespoon = one 15 ml spoon
1 teaspoon = one 5 ml spoon

2. Both metric and imperial measurements have been given in all recipes. Use one set of measurements only and not a mixture of both.

3. Eggs should be size 3 unless otherwise stated.

4. Milk should be full-fat unless otherwise stated.

5. Fresh herbs should be used unless otherwise stated. If unavailable use dried herbs as an alternative but halve the quantities stated.

6. Ovens should be preheated to the specified temperature – if using a fan assisted oven, follow manufacturer's instructions for adjusting the temperature.

7. All microwave information is based on a 650 watt oven. Follow manufacturer's instructions for an oven with a different wattage.

First published in Great Britain in 1994 by Hamlyn, an imprint of Reed Consumer Books Limited
Michelin House, 81 Fulham Road, London SW3 6RB
and Auckland, Melbourne, Singapore and Toronto

Text and illustrations copyright © 1994 IPC Magazines Limited, except for photographs pp 6, 8, 9, 11 and 15 copyright © Reed International Books Limited/Sandra Lousada
Design copyright © 1994 Reed International Books Limited

Reprinted 1994

ISBN 0 600 578 33X

A CIP catalogue record for this book is available from the British Library

Produced by Mandarin Offset
Printed and bound in Hong Kong

ACKNOWLEDGEMENTS

Editor: Jo Lethaby
Designer: Alyson Kyles

PRACTICAL PARENTING
ACKNOWLEDGEMENTS:

Editor: Helen Gill
Deputy Editor: Jane Kemp
Cookery Editor: Sara Lewis
Photographers: Dave Jordan, James Duncan, Steve Lee and Tony Robins

C·O·N·T·E·N·T·S

H·E·A·L·T·H

& N·U·T·R·I·T·I·O·N

Since your child's early eating habits will probably set a pattern for life, a healthy and balanced diet is important right from the start, whether your child loves snacking, prefers three hearty meals a day, or appears to eat very little. Here we guide you from preparing a baby's first tiny tastes to catering for hungry pre-schoolers.

STARTING ON SOLIDS

The first tiny mouthful of solid food heralds a whole new adventure for both you and your baby. As you wean her from milk to mixed food you are not only introducing your baby to wonderful new tastes and textures but also to an important part of social and family life.

Just as you and your baby helped each other establish breast or bottlefeeding, so you will eventually make the progression from sloppy spoonfuls to family meals. Weaning takes place gradually over weeks and months. Your baby will set the pace, so don't rush her; simply help her to enjoy food and try to make mealtimes as fun and relaxed as possible.

When to wean your baby

There's no right time to wean. Every baby is different – some thrive on milk feeds alone until they are five or six months old, others are hungrier and start demanding solids at three or four months. But it's recommended that you don't start earlier than three or four months and leave it no later than six months. If you start your baby on solids before she's ready, her digestive system may not be mature enough to cope with the demands of real food. It may also increase her vulnerability to allergies – especially if there is a family history of this. From the age of six months your baby needs the valuable iron found in solid foods that is not provided by milk. Late weaning will also make it harder for your child to adjust to chewing and biting.

Your baby will let you know when milk is no longer enough to satisfy her growing appetite. The following signs indicate that it may be time to start weaning:

• she sucks her fists or takes an interest in what you eat
• she demands more after a good milk feed
• she finds it hard to settle at night or wakes for an extra feed
• she wants more and more feeds during the day.

You'll probably pick up these signals from your baby yourself but if you have any doubts about when to start weaning, then do ask your health visitor for advice.

Getting started

The best time to give the first spoonful of solids is when your baby is feeling cheerful and alert. She should be ready for food but not so hungry that only milk will do. The lunchtime feed is usually a good time to begin on solids. It's also important that you are feeling relaxed, with plenty of time to sit down with your baby. This can be a very demanding stage and you're going to need a lot of patience at first to cope with the inevitable dribbling and mess!

It helps to see things from your baby's point of view. Until now she has only had food in familiar liquid form which comes in a continuous stream and requires little effort to take. Eating solids is an altogether different sensation and your baby will need time and reassurance to help her adjust. Not only is the taste and texture completely different, but she'll be practising a new set of skills as she takes the food from the spoon to the back of her mouth and swallows.

To help make your baby feel more secure, give her most of her milk feed first to take the edge off her hunger and then offer a tiny amount of solids. Hold your baby on your lap and talk to her as you do so. It's best to use a special plastic weaning spoon which is small and shallow so she can suck the food off with her lips. Place the spoon gently between her lips, but don't be surprised if she turns her head away or spits the food out – she needs time to get used to it. Once she has tried a spoonful you can offer her more breast or formula milk if she's still hungry. Try giving another spoonful of solids at the same time the following day and gradually your baby will become accustomed to taking solids.

If she really doesn't seem to like it she may not be ready yet, so give it a rest for a few days and

H·E·A·L·T·H & N·U·T·R·I·T·I·O·N

small pieces. Place them in a saucepan and add just enough water to cover (don't add salt or any other seasonings) and simmer until tender. Alternatively, steam the fruit or vegetables for about 10 minutes or until soft but not mushy. Drain or remove from the steamer, keeping the cooking water, then blend or mash very well to remove any lumps. If the purée is too thick you can add some cooking water, breast or formula milk or unsweetened fruit juice to thin it down a little. This will make the purée easier for your baby to swallow; if it's too thick it will stick to the roof of her mouth and she'll find it difficult to swallow. As she gets used to the texture, decrease the amount of liquid to make it thicker.

How much to give

For the first week or so offer your baby one or two spoonfuls of solids at one meal during the day. When she's taking this happily you can slowly increase the amount of food and add an extra meal – perhaps giving a little cereal at breakfast and then a purée at lunchtime. By six to eight months of age she may be taking three or four meals a day. Her appetite may vary from day to day, so let her take the lead. She'll let you know when she's had enough to eat by closing her mouth, turning her head away or spitting out the food.

You may worry that your baby isn't getting enough to eat during these early months but she's still getting all her basic nutritional requirements from breast or formula milk. In the early days solids are a stepping stone to introducing your child to real food so she becomes familiar with the different tastes and textures, until solids gradually replace breast or bottlefeeds.

Once your baby is taking a few spoonfuls of first foods you can try introducing new flavours. Try cooked and puréed cauliflower, potato or pear, or well-mashed ripe banana. Introduce new foods one at a time and allow a day or so before you try them again. Some babies are upset by certain foods; others show a positive dislike

then try again. Never offer your baby solids from a bottle because of the danger of choking. Your baby also needs to learn how to take food from a spoon so she can experience different textures and have the opportunity to refuse what she doesn't want or need.

First tastes

Your baby's first taste of solid food should be very bland and easy to swallow. Try baby rice diluted with expressed breast or formula milk, cooled boiled water or unsalted cooking liquid to make it semi-liquid. Or make a purée of mild-flavoured fruit or vegetables such as carrot, parsnip or apple which are fairly sweet and mild. First foods should be served lukewarm since babies' mouths are very sensitive to temperature and can be easily burned.

To make puréed first foods, wash fruit or vegetables thoroughly then peel and cut into for particular flavours. By introducing foods gradually you will be able to see which ones your baby prefers. If your baby reacts badly to certain foods – perhaps by having unusually dirty or smelly nappies – leave them off the menu for a few weeks before trying again. At this early stage it's helpful to keep a weaning diary so you can note down any likes and dislikes.

Occasionally, babies are allergic to foods with various reactions ranging from vomiting to skin rashes. The most common culprits are cow's milk and other dairy products, eggs, fish, citrus fruits, foods containing gluten and artificial food colourings and additives. To be on the safe side it's best to avoid these until your baby is between six and nine months old (see *What foods to give when*, page 10). There's no need to worry too much about infant food allergies but if either you or your partner have an allergy or you have any concerns then you should consult your health visitor or doctor.

Once your baby is used to a few different foods you can start combining flavours to add variety and create interesting mini-meals. Try swede, turnip and parsnip, apple and banana or courgette and potato. You can mix sweet with savoury flavours but don't be too adventurous – babies have very bland tastebuds and actually enjoy a bit of monotony! If your baby shows an obvious dislike for a certain food, don't make a fuss. Take it away and try again in a few weeks.

Once your child is enjoying several spoonfuls of solids at her meals you can start cutting down on the milk at one meal, perhaps at midday, and replace it with cooled boiled water. Take your cue from your baby who will start dropping milk feeds naturally in favour of solids. It's important to offer your child plenty to drink to avoid dehydration, especially on hot days, but don't give her any sweetened or fizzy drinks which can lead to tooth decay even before your baby's first teeth appear.

H·E·A·L·T·H & N·U·T·R·I·T·I·O·N

WHAT FOODS TO GIVE WHEN

Every baby develops at her own pace so these suggestions can only be guidelines. Don't rush your baby – wait until you feel she is ready to progress to the next stage.

4-6 months
Texture: semi-liquid, blended, puréed, sieved, no lumps, pips or strings.
Try: puréed vegetables and fruit – potato, carrots, peas, cauliflower, marrow, swede, pumpkin, celery, parsnip, apple, pear, banana, peach, plum, melon. Non-wheat (gluten-free) cereals such as baby rice, thinned with breast or formula milk, cooled boiled water or non-salted cooking water.
Drink: breast or formula milk, cooled boiled water, very diluted unsweetened fruit juice.

6-8 months
Texture: finely minced and mashed. Add liquid if necessary. Still fairly soft but with small 'bits', no pips, strings or bones. Introduce finger foods and experiment with different flavours.
Add: chicken, turkey, white fish (skinned, boned and flaked), bread, yogurt and mild hard cheese, liver, sweetcorn, cheese, tomatoes (skinned and sieved). Breakfast cereals such as porridge, Ready Brek or Weetabix (choose one that is low in sugar and salt). Breads, crispbreads, rusks.
Drink: breast or formula milk. Start introducing a cup or beaker for other liquids. Avoid sugary or fizzy drinks.

8-9 months
Texture: chopped, grated, much coarser and more chewy. Plenty of finger foods.
Add: pasta, rice, split peas, butter beans, lentils, lean red meats, hard-boiled egg yolk, dried fruit

(softened by soaking in boiled water).
Drink: your baby will be taking less breast or formula milk now so offer other drinks such as water or diluted unsweetened fruit juice. Try making your own fruit and vegetable drinks.

10-12 months
Texture: bite-sized pieces. Vary the consistency of foods.
Add: stronger-flavoured vegetables such as broccoli, leeks, onions, cabbage, tinned fish (drained and flaked), oily fish such as mackerel and tuna, citrus fruits, berry fruits (put through the hand-mill to get rid of pips and seeds), well-cooked pork, egg white.
Drink: solids are now the major part of your baby's diet but she stills needs at least one pint of whole milk per day. Give plenty of other liquids.

Milk feeds

Don't cut back on milk too quickly as your baby needs the essential nutrients provided in ideal proportions in milk. Up to the age of five months your baby should be having at least four milk feeds a day. Until she's at least one year old your baby should still be having around a pint of milk a day – either as milk or in dairy products – since it's one of the major sources of energy for a growing child.

Preparing first foods

You don't need any special equipment to prepare food for your baby. The basic items are a fork for mashing, a sieve for removing pips and bones, and a grater. A small food blender or processor or a hand-held food mill are ideal for puréeing small quantities. When preparing food for young babies it's essential to wash your hands well and keep everything scrupulously clean. Until your baby is six months old her bottles must be sterilized if she's using them for milk feeds.

Although it's not essential to sterilize feeding equipment for solid food, you may want to do this. Clean spoons and dishes can be immersed in cold water with a sterilizing tablet or fluid, usually for at least half an hour. The water should be changed every day, and the items rinsed in boiled water before use. Alternatively, you can boil the necessary equipment for 20 minutes, or use a steam sterilizer.

Baby foods can be cooked in a variety of ways – boiling, steaming, stewing or baking – but avoid frying or roasting as this makes the food very fatty and difficult for babies to digest.

Cooking in such small quantities can be very fiddly so save time and effort by freezing meal-sized portions. Some foods such as bananas and avocados don't freeze, but most other foods freeze quite well. Cook and purée the food, cover, leave to cool and then freeze until solid in handy-sized ice-cube trays or plastic pots. Turn out and store the frozen purée in freezer bags until you need a

baby meal. Always reheat thoroughly, cool then serve immediately. It's recommended that you don't use a microwave because of the danger of hot spots in the centre of the food.

There are a variety of commercially prepared baby foods on the market. These are convenient especially when you are very busy or when travelling but they can be expensive, especially if your baby is still eating very small quantities. Spoon out the required amount only, as unused baby food should never be reheated. These baby foods are nutritionally well balanced, however, and many parents prefer them to making their own baby food. When buying commercially prepared baby meals, do read the labels carefully to ensure they are the right age and stage for your child, that there is no added salt, artificial flavourings or colourings and that the sugar content is low – this may appear as sucrose, fructose or maltodextrin.

H·E·A·L·T·H & N·U·T·R·I·T·I·O·N

FIRST FOODS TO FAMILY MEALS

This is an exciting, albeit wonderfully messy stage as your baby tackles the art of feeding herself. It takes a lot of practice to master the necessary skills and co-ordination. Your child will inevitably make a mess, but you can limit it by putting a plastic sheet or newspaper on the floor and covering her clothes with a bib. Plastic bibs with a lip for catching scraps are especially useful.

By six to eight months old, your child will be starting to cope with more solid food and enjoying a wider variety of tastes. Serve food that is mashed and diced to encourage chewing at this early stage. You can start to introduce white meats and fish, bread and rusks and cheese and yogurt. It is recommended, however, that you avoid giving your baby fresh cow's milk to drink until she is one year old.

Around this time she'll probably start grabbing for the spoon as you try to feed her. It's a good idea to encourage this independence by giving her a spoon to hold. At first she'll probably enjoy dipping it into the food and trying to get it into her mouth, although most of it is likely to end up on her clothes or the floor. She may like to put her hands into her bowl too, and spread the food around her face. Let her enjoy playing with her food – it's all part of the learning process. You can give her a thorough wash after the meal!

By around eight months your baby will enjoy eating foods with her fingers, another step towards independent eating. Pieces of baked bread, pasta or raw vegetables are ideal for sucking and gnawing but make sure there is no danger that they will break off in her mouth. Finger foods are great for exercising jaws and gums, and are especially comforting during teething. She may enjoy sticks of carrot, cucumber or apple as a healthy snack.

However confident your child appears to be with eating, never be tempted to leave her alone with food because of the danger of choking. For the same reason, avoid giving her whole nuts, fruit with stones, whole grapes and similar foods which could get stuck in her throat.

Preparing family meals

As your baby's feeding skills develop so will her appetite. By around eight or nine months, your child will probably be having three meals a day. She will be old enough to sit in a highchair and may have cut a few teeth. She is starting to feed herself and drink from a beaker. Now is the right time to start arranging mealtimes to fit in with the rest of the family.

Eating together will save having to cook two separate meals as your baby can eat almost all the meals you usually prepare for the family, apart from tough meats, rich sauces and strong seasonings. It's best to keep the salt, fat and sugar content low or to set aside a portion for your baby before adding seasoning.

Healthy cooking tips

Follow these guidelines when preparing meals for your baby.

Salt: Your baby's kidneys are still too young to cope with too much salt, and there's plenty naturally present in food. Leave out salt when cooking for your baby. You don't need to add any to boiling water for vegetables, and shouldn't use salty foods and ingredients such as stock cubes and gravy thickeners. As your child grows older, try to avoid giving her too many salty snacks such as crisps and similar snacks.

Sugar: Too much sugar can lead to dental decay even before the teeth start coming through. There's enough natural sugar to be found in milk, fruit and vegetables. Don't add sugar to cereals or stewed fruit.

Spices and highly seasoned foods: Children find spices and strong seasonings hard to digest until they are over two years old.

Fatty foods: Milk provides all the energy that your child needs. Go easy on serving fatty meats, cream, ice-cream, pastry and fried foods.

Food fads

Some time after her first birthday your child will probably start having particular likes and dislikes for food, perhaps refusing to eat anything but jam sandwiches or fish fingers and tomato ketchup for days on end. She may seem to eat very little or eat too much. For parents, these fads can be very worrying. Sooner or later she'll pick up on your natural concern about her diet and discover that food is a wonderful weapon for manipulating you.

This stage is very common but it will pass. If your child looks healthy, has plenty of energy and sleeps well then she's probably getting all the nutrients she needs.

Try to adopt a calm and flexible attitude to what she eats and how she eats it. If she sees that her behaviour isn't making any impact then she may give up. You can't control her eating but you can control your reactions, so if you feel yourself getting upset try not to coax or bribe her. Make as little fuss as possible – it won't hurt her to miss the occasional meal.

H·E·A·L·T·H & N·U·T·R·I·T·I·O·N

Stay-calm tactics for mealtimes:

• Sit down with your child when she eats. Try to have something to eat or drink, even if it's only a cup of tea. If you can eat the same as her then so much the better.

• Try not to rush her when she's eating – give her time and keep mealtimes fun.

• Make sure your child is comfortable and the chair is at the right height. If she's sitting on a booster seat she must be able to reach her plate easily. Check that her cutlery is the right size for her small hands.

• Keep meals as simple and effortless as possible. If she throws it on the floor or turns up her nose in disgust, you won't then find yourself feeling resentful or rejected.

• Keep rules to a minimum. Until your child has mastered the art of eating with a spoon and fork and drinking from a cup there are bound to be spills and mess. Don't worry too much about manners at this stage and let her eat with her fingers if she wants.

• Give small portions – too much food piled on a plate can be very off-putting. She can always ask for more if she's hungry. Alternatively, place food in a dish on the table and let your child serve herself a little at a time.

• Pay attention to colour and texture to add plenty of variety and give the meal instant appeal. Arrange fruit and vegetables in different patterns; make face shapes and pinwheel sandwiches. Give small piles of individual foods rather than mixing them all up.

• Respect your child's likes and dislikes. If she doesn't like cooked vegetables, try serving them raw instead. Choose meals that are based on her favourite foods. Try offering one new food at a time, but don't insist that she eats anything she doesn't like.

• Let your child have some choice by offering a limited number of alternatives. If she wants to experiment with different flavours give her the opportunity – peanut butter and banana sandwiches may not sound appetizing to you but it's better to allow her some say in what she chooses to eat.

• Involve your child in food preparation and mealtimes – let her help by putting out cutlery, washing vegetables or weighing ingredients when you're cooking.

• Chat to your child while you are preparing food – look at colours and ingredients together, let her feel all the different textures and take tiny tastes of any new foods. She can have hours of fun cutting out pastry shapes and making patterns with pasta.

How to help a faddy eater:

Many parents worry that their child seems to have a poor appetite, but if you note down everything that your child eats and drinks in a week you'll probably be pleasantly surprised at the amount and variety she consumes. If you are still concerned, however, note the following tips:

• Make an effort to serve meals at regular intervals so that she isn't too tired to eat.

• Remember that children usually prefer simple foods. Don't try mixing too many different flavours at any meal.

• Children soon get bored with casseroles – serve individual foods instead.

• Try serving meals in different surroundings – perhaps in the garden or in a make-shift 'café' at home. You may find that your child will eat better at someone else's house – maybe a friend's or a relative's.

• Cut out snacks and drinks between meals. There are a surprising number of calories in snacks, milk and fruit juices, so your child may not be hungry when it comes to mealtimes. Offer a drink at the end of the meal so that it doesn't fill her up beforehand.

• Invent new names for dishes and encourage your child to give different vegetables a special name, or call certain foods after favourite people or television characters.

H·E·A·L·T·H & N·U·T·R·I·T·I·O·N

If your child eats too much

Try to arrange your child's diet so she's unlikely to develop weight problems later in life. Your health visitor will tell you if there is any cause for concern. Your child still needs plenty of nourishment so don't take drastic measures even if she is overweight, but you can easily make the following simple adjustments to limit the excess calories:

- Restrict between-meal snacks and substitute fresh fruit and vegetables for sweets and crisps.
- Don't add sugar to foods, avoid canned sweetened fruit, and keep biscuits, cakes and sweets for special occasions.
- Serve water or diluted unsweetened fruit juice instead of sugary drinks.
- Cut down on fatty fried foods such as chips – steam, bake or boil instead.
- Provide plenty of fresh food rather than processed foods.
- Increase the amount of exercise your child takes by playing games in the garden or park.
- Don't worry if your child eats the wrong things occasionally, for example at parties – it's her overall intake of food that is important.

GIVING A WELL-BALANCED DIET

To help you plan menus and snacks, food can be divided into various groups.

Give generous helpings of foods from the two groups below:

Cereals and grains: this includes bread, pasta, rice and oats. These foods are high in energy content and provide vitamins and minerals. It's a good idea to start introducing wholegrain bread and cereals which contain fibre, but don't overdo them as children may find it hard to cope with too much roughage. Never add bran to a child's food. Starchy foods such as potatoes are also high in energy and are best served simply, either baked, steamed, boiled or mashed.

Vegetables and fruit: fresh or frozen. Preferably raw or freshly cooked. Avoid tinned fruit in sugary syrup and tinned vegetables in salt. Try to include at least two helpings of vegetables per day and up to four helpings or pieces of fruit. Certain husked and fibrous vegetables may arrive undigested in the nappy – this is perfectly normal. If your child doesn't like vegetables you can try disguising them in puréed soups or mixed in with dishes such as macaroni cheese, lasagne or spaghetti bolognaise. You may find she prefers raw vegetables or fruit and will enjoy home-made vegetable and fruit drinks made in a blender. Mix them with water or milk, and experiment to find a consistency your child likes. A bendy straw also helps, too!

Give smaller amounts each day from the following two groups:

Meat and alternatives: such as poultry, fish, eggs, nuts (ground, not whole) and lentils, beans and peas. Choose white meats and fish rather than red meats and select lean cuts of meat.

Milk, cheese and yogurt: use whole milk until your child is at least two years old. You may then wish to change to semi-skimmed if your child is getting all the energy she needs from her diet. Choose mild hard cheeses or cottage cheese and pasteurized whole milk yogurt (unsweetened is best; add your own fruit if you wish).

Keep foods from these two groups to a minimum:

Fats and oils: children need some fat in their diet, but it's important not to have too much saturated fat which comes mainly from animal sources. Grill, steam or bake food, serve lean meat and spread margarine or butter thinly on toast and in sandwiches.

Sugar, sugary foods and drinks: these contain empty calories and may take away your child's appetite for more nutritious food. Of course, there's nothing wrong with the odd sweet treat, but keep them for certain days or times, such as after lunch.

H·E·A·L·T·H & N·U·T·R·I·T·I·O·N

DAILY MEAL PLANNER

Include at least two servings of protein (meat, poultry, fish, eggs, dairy products), at least four helpings of fruit and vegetables, and four or more servings of bread and cereal (½ slice of bread or 1 tbsp of cereal is one serving). Your child should drink one pint of whole milk a day.

These daily menu suggestions will help you to give your child a well-balanced diet:

Breakfast
• plain cereal with milk and no extra sugar
• toasted wholemeal bread, lightly buttered
• milk

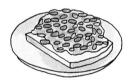

Lunch
• light meal such as cheese or baked beans on toast, baked potato or pasta with cheese, grilled fish fingers and peas, sardine sandwich, cold cooked meat with tomato and cucumber
• one piece of fresh fruit
• milk or diluted fruit juice or water

Main meal
• one serving of lean meat, poultry or fish, grilled or baked
• one portion of pasta, rice or potatoes (boiled, steamed, baked or mashed)
• one portion of fresh vegetables
• fresh fruit, yogurt, milk pudding, fromage frais, ice-cream

Bedtime
• a warm, milky drink

VITAMINS AND MINERALS

Children who enjoy a wide variety of foods should be getting all the essential vitamins and minerals. However, if your child is a very fussy eater or you have any other concerns about their diet, ask your doctor or health visitor about supplements. The important vitamins and minerals are:

Vitamin A
Necessary for: protection from infection, growth, strong bones and teeth, healthy eyes, skin and gums.

Found in: oily fish, liver, dairy products, yellow or dark green vegetables, apricots, butter and eggs.

Vitamin B
Necessary for: growth, converting food into energy, healthy nervous system and digestion.

Found in: meat, especially liver, yeast extract (such as Marmite), fish, dairy produce and eggs, wholegrain cereals, wheatgerm, dried beans, dark green vegetables and bananas.

Vitamin C
Necessary for: growth, healthy bones, teeth and gums, healing of wounds and absorption of iron.

Found in: raw or lightly cooked vegetables and fruit, especially citrus fruits, blackcurrants, strawberries, potatoes, green peppers and leafy green vegetables.

Vitamin D
Necessary for: healthy bones and teeth.

Found in: fortified margarine, oily fish, liver, oils, egg yolk, fortified breakfast cereals and dairy produce. Produced naturally in skin exposed to sunlight.

Vitamin E
Necessary for: strong muscles; helps the body to create and maintain red blood cells.

Found in: vegetable oils, margarine, wholegrain cereals, wheatgerm, dried beans, leafy green vegetables and nuts (ground, not whole).

Vitamin K
Necessary for: blood clotting.
Found in: vegetables and wholegrain cereals.

Calcium
Necessary for: healthy bones and teeth; helps blood to clot.

Found in: milk and other dairy produce, canned fish with soft bones (sardines and salmon), dried beans, citrus fruit and leafy green vegetables.

Iron
Necessary for: making haemoglobin, the oxygen-carrying pigment in red blood cells (iron deficiency can lead to anaemia).

Found in: red meat, liver, oily fish, egg yolks, dried fruits (especially apricots), wholegrain cereals, pulses and green leafy vegetables.

STILL HUNGRY?
Even with three good meals a day, energetic children may still need something to fill the gap. If your child is hungry between meals try offering:
- Fresh fruit – seedless grapes, satsumas and bananas are quick and easy to eat, or chop up apples or pears
- Filled rolls, sandwiches or pitta bread

- Yogurts or milk shakes
- Home-made popcorn (no salt or sugar)
- Breadsticks or rusks
- Pasta pieces with a little grated cheese

VEGETARIAN CHOICE
Babies and children can thrive on a vegetarian diet and there's plenty of choice available these days. However, it's especially important to ensure that your child is getting enough iron and protein-rich foods. Offer well-cooked, mashed pulses and rice, ground nut pastes, vegetarian cheese, and plenty of dairy products and eggs (unless you are vegans in which case your child may need vitamin supplements). Soya flour and soya products are packed with nutrients and can be used in a variety of ways.

All the recipes in this book have been tried and tested by readers of *Practical Parenting* and their children, and will help you to provide well-balanced and imaginative meals for your whole family.

· C H A P T E R 1 ·

F·I·R·S·T
F·O·O·D·S

Making your own baby food from fresh, natural ingredients is a cheap and healthy way to feed your baby. Make enough for several meals in one go and freeze them to cut down on the preparation time when you want to feed your baby. We've also included some tempting recipes for your toddler.

SUNSHINE CHICKEN

MAKES: 7 baby portions

1 onion, finely chopped
550 g (1¼ lb) potatoes, peeled
  and diced
325 g (12 oz) carrots, peeled
  and diced
3 chicken thighs
100 g (4 oz) red lentils
300 ml (½ pint) water
150 ml (¼ pint) cow's or
  formula milk
1 bay leaf
To serve:
broccoli and cauliflower florets

PREPARATION: 20 minutes
COOKING: 1 hour

1. Preheat the oven to 180°C, 350°F, Gas 4. Place the onion, potatoes and carrots in a flameproof casserole.
2. Rinse chicken and lentils, drain and add both to the casserole with the water, milk and bay leaf. Bring to the boil, cover and cook in the oven for 1 hour, or until chicken is thoroughly cooked. To check, pierce with a skewer; if juices are clear, chicken is ready.
3. Remove from heat. Remove bay leaf and discard. Lift chicken out of mixture with a slotted spoon. Remove skin with a fork and discard bones. Return meat to casserole.
4. Mash or purée the mixture, depending on age of child, adding extra milk if needed. Cover and cool.
To freeze: pack into small jars, plastic boxes or ice-cube trays. Seal, label and freeze for up to 2 months.
To thaw: microwave for 1½-2 minutes for three ice cubes or 2½-3 minutes for a jar on Full Power (100%). Stir well. Or defrost in fridge overnight then transfer to a saucepan and bring to the boil, stirring. Check the temperature before serving with steamed broccoli and cauliflower florets.

Left: Sunshine Chicken served with broccoli and cauliflower

Above: Liver & Bacon Hotpot served with apple slices and carrot sticks

LIVER & BACON HOTPOT

MAKES: 7 baby portions

1 leek, trimmed
325 g (12 oz) calf's liver
325 g (12 oz) potatoes, peeled and finely chopped
450 g (1 lb) swede, peeled and finely chopped
150 g (6 oz) carrots, peeled and finely chopped
2 rashers back bacon, derinded and chopped
300 ml (½ pint) water
2 tbsp tomato ketchup
To serve:
apple slices
carrot sticks

PREPARATION: 25 minutes
COOKING: 25 minutes

1. Slit leek lengthways and rinse well, shaking dry. Rinse liver, drain. Trim and chop.
2. Put potatoes, swede and carrots into saucepan with bacon, water and ketchup. Bring to the boil, cover and simmer for 15 minutes.
3. Add leek and liver, mix well; cover and cook for 10 minutes more, stirring occasionally. Mash or purée depending on age of child. Cover and cool.

To freeze: pack into small jars, plastic boxes or ice-cube trays. Seal, label and freeze for up to 2 months.

To thaw: microwave for 1½-2 minutes for three ice cubes or 2½-3 minutes for a jar on Full Power (100%). Stir well. Or defrost overnight in the fridge, transfer to a saucepan and bring to the boil, stirring. Check temperature before serving to baby with apple slices and carrot sticks.

F·I·R·S·T F·O·O·D·S

CHEESY MIXED VEGETABLES

MAKES: 10 baby portions

675 g (1½ lb) potatoes, peeled and diced
325 g (12 oz) broccoli, broken into florets
½ cauliflower, broken into florets
150 ml (¼ pint) water
300 ml (½ pint) cow's or formula milk
100 g (4 oz) Cheddar cheese, grated
To serve:
Cheddar cheese sticks
carrot sticks
baby corn cobs

PREPARATION: 20 minutes
COOKING: 15 minutes

1. Put vegetables into a saucepan with the water and milk. Bring to the boil, cover and simmer for 15 minutes or until they're tender, stirring occasionally.

2. Stir in cheese until melted then mash or purée, depending on age of child, adding extra milk if needed. Cover and cool.

To freeze: pack into small jars, plastic boxes or ice-cube trays. Seal, label and freeze for up to 2 months.

To thaw: microwave for 1½-2 minutes for three ice cubes or 2½-3 minutes for a jar on Full Power (100%). Stir well. Or defrost in fridge overnight, transfer to a saucepan and bring to the boil, stirring. Check temperature before serving with cheese and carrot sticks and baby corn cobs.

P·R·A·C·T·I·C·A·L·I·T·I·E·S

- Home-made baby meals can be kept in the fridge for up to 24 hours.
- Don't reheat baby meals more than once and throw away any food that is left over after a meal.

Top right: Mini Kebabs
Below: Cheesy Mixed Vegetables

CHICKEN STIR-FRY

SERVES: 2

*6 tbsp frozen stir-fry
  vegetables*
1 tsp oil
*1 chicken thigh, boned,
  skinned and finely diced*
2 tsp tomato ketchup
2 tbsp cooked rice
2 tbsp water

PREPARATION: 5 minutes
COOKING: 9 minutes

1. Put frozen vegetables into a
sieve, rinse with hot water to
defrost, then drain.
2. Heat the oil in a saucepan.
Add chicken and fry for 3 minutes, stirring until browned.
3. Add vegetables and fry for
4 minutes, stirring.
4. Add tomato ketchup, rice
and water to the pan, mix
together and cook for 2 minutes.
Cool slightly before serving.

Chicken Stir-fry

MINI KEBABS

SERVES: 2

*4 baby new potatoes,
  scrubbed and halved*
3 slices courgette, halved
2 button mushrooms, halved
4 cocktail sausages
2 tbsp frozen sweetcorn

PREPARATION: 6 minutes
COOKING: 10 minutes

1. Cook potatoes in a saucepan
of boiling water for 10 minutes.
2. Preheat the grill. Thread
the halved courgette slices and
mushrooms alternately on to
two skewers, along with the
cocktail sausages.
3. Cover the grill rack with a
piece of foil. Place kebabs on
foil and grill for 8-10 minutes,
turning several times until
sausages are browned.

4. Meanwhile, add the
sweetcorn to the potatoes for
the last 2 minutes. Drain.
5. Leave the vegetables and
kebabs to cool slightly, then
remove skewers. If your child
prefers small pieces of food,
then finely chop before serving.

F·I·R·S·T F·O·O·D·S

FISH & CHIPS

SERVES: *2*

10 alphabet oven chips
1 plaice fillet
knob of butter
6 tbsp breadcrumbs
3 tbsp grated Edam or
  mild Cheddar cheese
1 egg, beaten
2 broccoli florets

PREPARATION: 10 minutes
COOKING: 10 minutes

1. Preheat grill and line the grill pan with foil. Add the chips to grill pan and cook for 10 minutes, turning once until they are browned.
2. Skin the fish fillet, cut in half lengthways and then into thin strips.
3. Place a knob of butter in the grill pan and melt gently.

4. Mix the breadcrumbs and grated cheese in a small dish. Place beaten egg in a separate small dish. Dip fish in egg then coat in crumb mixture. Place in the grill pan.
5. Grill for 5 minutes, until crumbs are browned and the fish is cooked.
6. Break broccoli into pieces and cook for 3 minutes. Drain.
7. Cool slightly before serving.

FISH SAVOURY

SERVES: *2*

100 g (4 oz) frozen cod
  portion
1 tbsp frozen peas
2 broccoli florets
212 g (7½ oz) can number
  spaghetti

PREPARATION: 5 minutes
COOKING: 12 minutes

1. Preheat grill and cover the grill rack with foil. Put fish on foil and grill for 10 minutes, turning once until cooked thoroughly.
2. Meanwhile, cook the peas and broccoli in a small saucepan of boiling water for 3 minutes, then drain.
3. Heat spaghetti in pan.
4. Break the fish into small pieces with a fork and add to the spaghetti with the peas and broccoli. Leave to cool slightly. If your child prefers a smoother texture, then blend in a food processor or mash the meal before serving.

P·R·A·C·T·I·C·A·L·I·T·I·E·S

- Since toddlers eat such small amounts, it's often worth preparing several portions at one time.
- When serving fish to children, always check carefully that there are no bones. Buy ready-skinned fish fillets or ask the fishmonger to do it for you.

Above: Fish Savoury
Left: Fish & Chips with broccoli

SUMMER FRUIT & KIWI SWIRL

MAKES: 10 baby portions

225 g (8 oz) frozen summer fruits
2 tbsp water
4 kiwi fruits, peeled and chopped
300 ml (½ pint) ready-to-serve custard
4 tbsp icing sugar
To serve:
banana slices
sponge finger biscuits

PREPARATION: 25 minutes
COOKING: 2 minutes

1. Cook summer fruits in 2 tbsp water for 5 minutes until soft. Cool.
2. Purée kiwi fruit in a liquidizer or food processor, then press through sieve. Discard all seeds.
3. Purée summer fruits in rinsed liquidizer or food processor and press through rinsed sieve. Discard seeds.
4. Add half the custard and half the icing sugar to each fruit mixture; whisk until totally smooth.
To freeze: pour kiwi and summer fruit mixtures into separate ice-cube trays. Freeze

Above: Summer Fruit & Kiwi Swirl served with sliced banana

until solid; transfer to a plastic bag, seal and label. May be frozen for up to 2 months.
To thaw: defrost two cubes of summer fruit purée and two cubes of kiwi fruit purée in a small dish for 1½-2 minutes on Full Power (100%). Or defrost for 4 hours at room temperature. Swirl mixtures together with a knife and serve with sliced bananas and sponge finger biscuits, if liked.

F·I·R·S·T F·O·O·D·S

APRICOT RICE PUDDING

MAKES: 7 baby portions

*100 g (4 oz) ready-to-eat
    dried apricots*
100 g (4 oz) flaked rice
*1.2 litres (2 pints) cow's or
    formula milk*
50 g (2 oz) caster sugar
To serve:
*pinch ground cinnamon,
    optional*
sponge finger biscuits
mini boxes raisins

PREPARATION: 5 minutes
COOKING: 25 minutes

1. Finely chop apricots, put in pan with rice, milk and sugar.
2. Bring to the boil, then simmer for 25 minutes, stirring occasionally until thick.
3. Purée or leave mixture as it is, depending on age of child. Cover and cool.
To freeze: pack into small jars, plastic boxes or ice-cube trays. Seal, label and freeze for up to 2 months.
To thaw: microwave for 1½-2 minutes for three ice cubes or 2½-3 minutes for a jar on Full Power (100%). Stir well. Or defrost in fridge overnight and bring to the boil in a saucepan, stirring. Check temperature before serving to baby. Sprinkle cinnamon on top, if liked, and serve with sponge finger biscuits and a mini box of raisins.

APPLE & ORANGE PURÉE

MAKES: 7 baby portions

1 orange
*1.1 kg (2½ lb) cooking apples,
    peeled, cored and thinly
    sliced*
75 g (3 oz) demerara sugar
To serve:
*Cheddar cheese, diced
rich tea finger biscuits*

PREPARATION: 20 minutes
COOKING: 15 minutes

1. Grate orange rind and squeeze juice.
2. Put apple slices, orange rind and juice into a saucepan with the sugar. Cover and cook over medium heat for 10 minutes,

*Above: Apricot Rice Pudding
served with sponge finger biscuits
and a mini box of raisins*
*Below: Apple & Orange Purée
served with diced cheese and a
finger biscuit*

stirring occasionally until the apple is pulpy.

3. Purée and sieve or leave mixture as it is, depending on age of child. Cover and cool.

To freeze: pack into small jars, plastic boxes or ice-cube trays. Seal, label and freeze for up to 2 months.

To thaw: microwave for 1½-2 minutes for three ice cubes or 2½-3 minutes for a jar on Full Power (100%). Stir well. Or defrost for 4 hours at room temperature then warm in a saucepan, stirring all the time. Check temperature before serving to baby with cheese and a finger biscuit.

CREAMY JUNKET

SERVES: 4

375 ml (13 fl oz) milk
125 ml (4 fl oz) single cream
1 tbsp caster sugar
few drops pink food colouring
1 tsp rennet essence
To serve:
whipped cream
drinking chocolate powder,
* for dusting*
sponge finger biscuits

PREPARATION: 5 minutes
(plus setting time)
COOKING: 3 minutes

1. Place milk, single cream and sugar in saucepan and heat gently, stirring all the time, until mixture is warm.
2. Remove from heat and add food colouring. Stir in rennet.

3. Pour junket into small dishes and leave to set (do not refrigerate).
4. Top with whipped cream and a dusting of drinking chocolate powder. Serve with sponge finger biscuits.

FRUITY FLOWERS

SERVES: 4

2 green eating apples
1 red eating apple
4 scoops strawberry ice-cream
2 kiwi fruit, peeled and sliced
4 strawberries, hulled and
* sliced*
2 black grapes, halved and
* deseeded*

PREPARATION: 20 minutes

1. Halve the green apples horizontally, cut a thin slice from each half and reserve.
2. Scoop out centres of apple halves to make four shells.
3. Quarter, core and cut red apple into segments.

Above: Creamy Junket served with sponge finger biscuits

4. Place each apple shell on a small plate and put a scoop of ice-cream into each. Cover with kiwi fruit slices, arrange red apple slices and strawberry slices around the top. Place a grape half in the centre.
5. Cut apple leaves and stalks from reserved green apple slices. Arrange below flower and serve immediately.

Below: Fruity Flowers

F·U·N S·N·A·C·K·S
& M·I·N·I M·E·A·L·S

*Turn everyday ingredients and food from your
storecupboard and freezer into fun and irresistible
snacks and mini meals that will delight your kids.
Perfect for lunchtimes or a light supper, these recipes
are ideal for tempting fussy eaters and they're
guaranteed to raise a smile!*

FAMILY BREADWINNERS

MAKES: 12

6 slices bread
2 eggs
4 tbsp milk
*15 g (½ oz) butter or
   margarine*
2 tbsp oil
To decorate:
2 slices processed cheese
2 slices ham
¼ red pepper
small piece cucumber
few slices carrot

PREPARATION: 30 minutes
COOKING: 10 minutes

1. Stamp out twelve people
shapes, two from each slice of
bread, using shaped cutters.
2. Beat the eggs and milk
together in a shallow dish.
3. Heat half the butter or
margarine with half the oil in
a frying pan.
4. Dip half the bread people, a
few at a time, into the egg
mix, turn over and dip the
other side. Fry 2-3 minutes
until browned on both sides.
5. Lift out figures and drain
on kitchen paper. Keep warm
while coating rest of the bread
people in egg and cooking in
remaining butter and oil.
6. Cut the clothes and features
from decoration ingredients,
arrange as shown. Serve warm.

Left: Family Breadwinners
Right: Three Little Pigs

THREE LITTLE PIGS

SERVES: 4-5

16 cocktail sausages
8 rashers streaky bacon,
  derinded
little tomato ketchup
50 g (2 oz) green beans,
  trimmed and cut into small
  pieces
100 g (4 oz) frozen sweetcorn
2 tbsp water
8 cherry tomatoes, halved
small piece red pepper
small piece cucumber

PREPARATION: 45 minutes
COOKING: 10 minutes

1. Separate sausages by cutting between the links.
2. Cut bacon rashers in half. Spread a little ketchup over half a rasher then wrap around a sausage. Place on grill rack.
3. Continue until all the sausages are wrapped. Grill for about 10 minutes, turning once, until evenly browned. Cool slightly.
4. Put beans into a bowl with the sweetcorn and water, cover with clingfilm, pierce with a fork and microwave for 2½ minutes on High (100%), or cook in a saucepan of boiling water until tender. Drain and cool slightly.

5. Arrange wrapped sausages on plates. Position tomato halves as heads, add sweetcorn eyes, tiny pieces of red pepper as mouths and green beans as the legs. Spoon the remaining sweetcorn on to plates as a path. Cut thin strips of cucumber peel and twist around a cocktail stick, remove stick and add curly tails to pigs.

P·R·A·C·T·I·C·A·L·I·T·I·E·S

• Children may try new foods if presented imaginatively.
• Don't get too frustrated if your child doesn't eat all her food. Children often need less food than you think.

PIZZA PEOPLE

SERVES: 2

2 muffins
3 tbsp Ragu sauce
50 g (2 oz) Cheddar cheese,
  grated
4 frozen peas
¼ small courgette, finely
  chopped
2 small strips red pepper
2 tiny pieces carrot
2 mushrooms, halved
small piece yellow pepper
small piece green pepper

PREPARATION: 15 minutes
COOKING: 10 minutes

1. Split muffins and toast
three halves, discarding the
fourth. Cut one muffin piece
in half to make two semicircles.
2. Spread muffins with Ragu
sauce and sprinkle with
cheese. Add peas to round
muffins for eyes, and press
courgette pieces into the top

for hair. Grill muffins until
the cheese has melted.
3. Arrange on serving plates as
shown. Add red pepper
mouths and carrot noses. Use
halved mushrooms for ears.
4. Cut yellow shirt collars and
two green ties from peppers
and press on to bodies of pizza
people. Leave to cool slightly
before serving.

TUNA BOATS

MAKES: 8

4 medium-sized potatoes,
  scrubbed
1 carrot, sliced
75 g (3 oz) frozen vegetables
25 g (1 oz) butter
2 tbsp milk
salt and freshly ground black
  pepper
75 g (3 oz) Cheddar cheese,
  grated
198 g (7 oz) can tuna, drained
4 slices processed cheese

PREPARATION: 15 minutes
COOKING: 1 hour

1. Preheat the oven to 220°C,
425°F, Gas 7. Prick potatoes
and bake for 1 hour or until
they are soft.
2. Cut carrot slices into fish

Above: Tuna Boats served with
carrot fish shapes
Left: Pizza People

shapes with a small knife.

3. Cook frozen vegetables in boiling water for 3 minutes.

4. Meanwhile, take potatoes out of oven, halve and scoop out centres. Mix with butter, milk and seasoning.

5. Stir grated cheese into potato with the tuna. Drain vegetables, add to potato mixture, then spoon into potato shells.

6. Halve cheese slices diagonally to make sails and secure on potato boats with cocktail sticks. Serve with carrot fish shapes.

SALMON OCTOPUS

MAKES: 8

450 g (1 lb) potatoes, peeled and cut into chunks
6 spring onions, trimmed and chopped
50 g (2 oz) butter
212 g (7½ oz) can red salmon, drained
1-2 tbsp fresh lemon juice
salt and freshly ground black pepper
1 egg
2 tbsp milk
75 g (3 oz) fresh breadcrumbs
3 tbsp oil
100 g (4 oz) green beans, trimmed
16 frozen peas
4 cherry tomatoes, halved

PREPARATION: 25 minutes
COOKING: 35 minutes

1. Cook potato chunks in a saucepan of lightly salted boiling water for about 12-15 minutes until soft. Drain and mash.

2. Fry the spring onions in a knob of butter until soft.

3. Discard the salmon skin and bones.

4. Beat the remaining butter, lemon juice and seasoning into potatoes. Stir in spring onions and salmon.

5. Divide mixture into eight and pat into burger shapes with floured hands.

6. Beat egg and milk together on a plate. Put breadcrumbs on a second plate. Coat each burger first in egg, and then in the breadcrumbs.

7. Heat half the oil in a frying pan, add four burgers and fry for 8-10 minutes, turning once, until golden brown. Drain and keep warm. Repeat with the remaining burgers.

8. Meanwhile, cook green beans in boiling water for 5 minutes. Add peas for last 2 minutes. Drain.

9. Arrange burgers on plates and add bean tentacles, pea eyes and a halved tomato for each nose.

Below: Salmon Octopus

F·U·N S·N·A·C·K·S & M·I·N·I M·E·A·L·S

FISHY VOL AU VENTS

MAKES: 12

500 g (1 lb 2 oz) packet puff pastry, chilled
beaten egg, for glazing
Filling:
150 g (6 oz) cod fillet
150 ml (¼ pint) milk
15 g (½ oz) butter
15 g (½ oz) plain flour
50 g (2 oz) frozen prawns, defrosted
50 g (2 oz) frozen sweetcorn, defrosted
salt and freshly ground black pepper
100 g (4 oz) green beans
12 frozen peas

PREPARATION: 35 minutes
COOKING: 15 minutes

1. Preheat the oven to 220°C, 425°F, Gas 7. Cut out a fish shape from a piece of greaseproof paper about 10 cm (4 inches) long. Roll out pastry and using paper fish as a guide, cut out twelve pastry fish. Cut a circle from the centre of each almost down to the base, but do not remove. Put pastry fish on a greased baking sheet.

2. Brush with beaten egg and cook for 8-10 minutes until risen and golden. Turn the oven off and keep the pastry fish warm.

3. Meanwhile put the fish and milk in a saucepan, cover and simmer for 8-10 minutes until fish flakes easily.

4. Lift fish out of the pan with a fish slice. Peel off skin and break into flakes, discarding bones. Strain milk and reserve.

5. Melt butter in a saucepan. Add flour then gradually stir in the reserved milk. Bring to the boil, stirring continuously until thickened and smooth.

6. Chop prawns and stir into white sauce with sweetcorn, season. Cook for 1 minute. Fold in fish and heat through.

7. Trim the green beans and cook in boiling water for 5 minutes, adding the peas for the last 2 minutes. Drain.

8. Put pastry fish on plates. Remove pastry circle from each, spoon in fish sauce. Add pea eyes and bean water reeds.

Below: Fishy Vol Au Vents

PRAWN TOASTS

SERVES: 3-4

200 g (7 oz) packet frozen
prawns, defrosted
2 tsp dried chopped chives or
parsley, optional
1 tbsp cornflour
1 egg white
salt and freshly ground black
pepper
3 slices multi-grain white
bread
2 tbsp sesame seeds
oil for frying
To serve:
cucumber sticks

PREPARATION: 10 minutes
(plus 30 minutes chilling)
COOKING: 5 minutes

1. Put prawns, herbs (if using),
cornflour, egg white and
seasoning into a food
processor and mix to a coarse
paste. Alternatively, finely
chop the prawns and mix in a
bowl with other ingredients.
2. Cut slices of bread in half
and spread with prawn paste.
Sprinkle with sesame seeds.
3. Put on a plate, cover with
clingfilm and chill for about
30 minutes.

Above: Prawn Toasts served
with cucumber sticks

4. Heat about 5 mm (¼ inch)
depth of oil in a large frying
pan. Carefully place 2-3 pieces
of bread, with prawn paste
side down, into oil and fry
until golden brown, then turn
over and cook the other side
until crispy.
5. Lift out and drain well on
kitchen paper. Repeat with
remaining bread. Cut slices in
half, arrange on plates, serve
warm with cucumber sticks.

FRENCH TOASTIES

MAKES: 10

5 slices bread
1 egg
2 tbsp milk
15 g (½ oz) butter or
margarine
1 tbsp oil
To serve:
mustard and cress
½ carrot, thinly sliced
20 sweetcorn kernels
3 frozen beans, thawed

PREPARATION: 10 minutes
COOKING: 8 minutes

1. Stamp out animal shapes from bread with biscuit cutters.
2. Beat egg and milk together in a shallow dish.
3. Heat butter or margarine and oil together in a frying pan. Dip a few shapes at a time into the egg mixture, then put into frying pan.
4. Cook for 2 minutes on each side until golden. Drain well and keep warm in the oven while cooking remainder.
5. Arrange a couple of French Toasties on a plate and decorate as shown.

Below: French Toasties

CRISPY CHICKEN CUPS

MAKES: 12

Cups:
12 thin slices white or brown
bread
40 g (1½ oz) butter
Filling:
25 g (1 oz) butter or
margarine
25 g (1 oz) plain flour
300 ml (½ pint) milk
salt and freshly ground black
pepper
75 g (3 oz) Cheddar cheese,
grated
100 g (4 oz) cooked chicken,
diced
100 g (4 oz) frozen
sweetcorn, defrosted
To serve:
grated cheese
steamed courgettes and
broccoli

PREPARATION: 15 minutes
COOKING: 15 minutes

1. Preheat the oven to 200°C, 400°F, Gas 6. Cut the bread into 6 cm (2½ inch) squares.
2. Melt the butter and brush over the bread. Press the bread, buttered side down, into sections of a twelve-hole bun tray. Brush the insides of the cups with the remaining melted butter.
3. Cook for 10-12 minutes until crispy and golden.
4. Meanwhile, make the filling. Melt the butter or margarine in a saucepan. Stir

*Above: Crispy Chicken Cups
and Crispy Veggie Cups*

in the flour then gradually add
the milk and bring to the boil,
stirring until thickened and
smooth. Season.

5. Stir in all of the remaining
ingredients and heat through.

6. Place bread cups on serving
plates and spoon in the filling.
Top with extra grated cheese
and serve with steamed
courgettes and broccoli.

CRISPY VEGGIE CUPS

Make cups and sauce as for
Crispy Chicken Cups but omit
the chicken and sweetcorn.
Defrost 100 g (4 oz) frozen
mixed vegetables and 50 g
(2 oz) frozen baby broad
beans. Stir into sauce and heat
through. Place bread cups on
serving plates, spoon in filling.
Sprinkle with a little grated
cheese and serve with steamed
courgettes and broccoli.

35

F·U·N S·N·A·C·K·S & M·I·N·I M·E·A·L·S

STICKY DRUMSTICKS

MAKES: 2

2 chicken drumsticks, skin
  removed
1 tbsp tomato ketchup
1 tsp clear honey
1 tsp oil
To serve:
sweetcorn
broccoli florets
halved cherry tomatoes

PREPARATION: 10 minutes
COOKING: 25 minutes

1. Arrange the drumsticks in a foil-lined tin. Mix the tomato ketchup, honey and oil together and brush well over the chicken.
2. Cook under a preheated grill for 25 minutes or until the juices run clear when the chicken is pierced with a knife. Cool slightly.
3. Serve the chicken with sweetcorn, broccoli florets and cherry tomatoes. Wrap some foil around the end of the drumsticks before serving.

SMILEY SHEPHERD'S PIE

MAKES: 6

1 carrot, peeled and diced
1 small onion, finely chopped
225 g (8 oz) extra lean
  minced beef
198 g (7 oz) can baked beans
3 tbsp tomato ketchup
4 tbsp water
250 g (9 oz) potatoes, peeled
  and diced
15 g (½ oz) butter or
  margarine
1 tbsp milk
To decorate:
mustard and cress
12 frozen peas, thawed
¼ red pepper, cored, deseeded
  and sliced

PREPARATION: 30 minutes
COOKING: 30 minutes

1. Reserve some pieces of diced carrot for decoration.
2. Dry-fry onion, carrot and mince in a non-stick saucepan, stirring occasionally, until the mince is evenly browned.
3. Add baked beans, ketchup and water. Bring to the boil, stirring. Reduce heat, cover and simmer for 30 minutes.
4. Meanwhile, cook potatoes in a saucepan of boiling water for 15 minutes until soft. Drain and mash with butter or margarine and milk.

Left: Sticky Drumsticks served
with sweetcorn, broccoli florets
and cherry tomatoes

Above: Smiley Shepherd's Pie
Right: Potato Butterflies

5. Divide the mince mixture between six ramekins or foil tartlet cases. Cover with the hot mashed potato and fluff up with a fork.

6. *To make ahead:* cool dishes well. Open-freeze until solid then wrap in clingfilm. Seal and label. Freeze for up to 3 months.

To defrost: thaw in fridge overnight and reheat in oven at 200°C, 400°F, Gas 6, for 25 minutes. Alternatively, microwave (but not if using foil cases) on Full Power (100%) for 6 minutes and leave to stand for 5 minutes.

7. Decorate each dish with mustard and cress for hair, pea eyes, a reserved carrot nose and a red pepper mouth.

POTATO BUTTERFLIES

MAKES: 6

450 g (1 lb) potatoes, peeled and cut into chunks
salt
25 g (1 oz) butter or margarine
50 g (2 oz) Cheddar cheese, grated
1 egg, beaten
6 sausages
½ carrot, scrubbed and thinly sliced
6 green beans, trimmed and halved
¼ red pepper, deseeded and diced
1 tbsp frozen or canned sweetcorn
1 tbsp frozen peas

PREPARATION: 15 minutes
COOKING: 35 minutes

1. Preheat the oven to 200°C, 400°F, Gas 6. Cook potato in lightly salted boiling water for 10-15 minutes until tender.

2. Drain and mash with butter or margarine. Beat cheese and egg into potato, making sure there are no lumps.

3. Spoon into a piping bag fitted with a large star nozzle.

4. Prick sausages and space well apart on a greased baking sheet. Pipe the potato into star shapes on each side of the sausages to form the butterfly wings.

5. Cook in the oven for 20 minutes until browned.

6. Meanwhile, cut carrot slices into twelve flower shapes with a small biscuit cutter.

7. Cook the carrot, beans and pepper in a small saucepan of boiling water for 3 minutes.

Add the sweetcorn and peas 1 minute before the end of cooking time.

8. Carefully transfer butterflies to serving plates, using a fish slice. Drain vegetables and serve butterflies as shown.

MUNCHING MICE

SERVES: 4-6

225 g (8oz) raspberries
65 g (2½ oz) caster sugar
1 tbsp gelatine
600 ml (1 pint) water
½ small melon
1 ripe pear, peeled, halved
and cored
few flaked almonds
chocolate polka dots
few raisins or grapes
thin strip of liquorice

PREPARATION: 20 minutes
COOKING: 5 minutes

1. Place raspberries, sugar, gelatine and 250 ml (8 fl oz) water in a food processor or blender. Blend until smooth.
2. Place in a saucepan with remaining water and bring to the boil, stirring. Pour into a large shallow dish and chill until set to make jelly.
3. Remove seeds from melon and cut away skin. Roughly shape a wedge from melon flesh, about 7.5 x 5 cm (3 x 2 inches) and cut out some small scoops using a melon baller, to resemble cheese.
4. Place melon on jelly with the pear halves flat side down. Stick flaked almonds into pears for ears, chocolate polka dots for mouths and small pieces of raisin or grape for eyes. Cut liquorice and curl up on jelly for mouse tails.

P·R·A·C·T·I·C·A·L·I·T·I·E·S

• Children need to eat fruit daily. Fruits canned in natural fruit juice make a good standby, if fresh fruit is unavailable.

Right: Sorbet Snail
Below: Munching Mice

SORBET SNAIL

SERVES: 4

150 g (6 oz) caster sugar
450 ml (¾ pint) water
2 x 425 g (15 oz) cans mango
  or peach slices in syrup
juice of ½ lemon
50 g (2 oz) plain chocolate
4 bananas
4 seedless grapes
1 apple, quartered, cored
  and sliced

PREPARATION: 30 minutes
(plus freezing overnight)
COOKING: 5 minutes

1. Put the caster sugar and water in a saucepan and heat gently, stirring occasionally until the sugar has dissolved. Boil for 5 minutes. Leave the syrup to cool.
2. Process or liquidize the mango or peach slices until puréed. Stir into the cooled syrup with the lemon juice. Pour into a plastic box and freeze for 4-5 hours or until the mixture is almost solid.
3. If the fruit mixture is very hard, leave at room temperature for 10 minutes to soften slightly. Process or liquidize in batches until the mixture is smooth. Then return to the plastic box and freeze again until solid.
4. Melt chocolate in a bowl over a pan of hot water and spoon into a piping bag. Scoop sorbet on to a plate, arrange a peeled banana to make snail's body. Pipe lines on to sorbet for snail's shell and pipe your child's name on to banana. Add a grape and apple slices to make the snail's head. Serve immediately. (Any sorbet that's left over after making snails' shells can be re-frozen.)

F·U·N S·N·A·C·K·S & M·I·N·I M·E·A·L·S

FUNNY FACE CLOWN

SERVES: 1

½ peach or nectarine, peeled
    and stone removed
1 pot fruit-flavoured fromage
    frais
jelly diamonds
1 glacé cherry
strips of peach, nectarine,
    orange or apple skin to
    decorate
1 wafer biscuit
1 Smartie or small sweet

PREPARATION: 10 minutes

1. Place the peach or nectarine half flat-side down on a plate.
2. Place the fromage frais in a piping bag fitted with a writing nozzle. Use to pipe the curly hair over the peach or nectarine face, and buttons and arms on the plate.
3. Use jelly diamonds for the eyes and collar, the cherry for the nose and fruit skin for the mouth and bow tie.
4. Position a triangle of wafer biscuit for the clown's hat with a small sweet at the top, secured in place with a blob of fromage frais.

Above: Funny Face Clown

CHOCOLATE & VANILLA BISCUITS

MAKES: 40 biscuits

100 g (4 oz) self-raising flour
15 g (½ oz) cocoa powder
50 g (2 oz) soft margarine
50 g (2 oz) caster sugar
1 tbsp golden syrup
Vanilla biscuits:
Ingredients as above
Omit cocoa powder and
    replace with 15 g (½ oz)
    self-raising flour
Few drops of vanilla essence
To decorate:
450 g (1 lb) icing sugar
2 tbsp water
pink, blue, yellow and green
    food colourings
4 greaseproof-paper piping
    bags
edible cake decorations

PREPARATION: 1 hour
COOKING: 12-15 minutes

1. Preheat the oven to 160°C, 325°F, Gas 3. For chocolate biscuits, sift flour and cocoa together in a bowl. Add margarine, cut into small pieces, and rub into the flour using fingertips until the mixture resembles fine breadcrumbs.

2. Stir in the caster sugar and golden syrup. Continue mixing until the crumbs begin to bind together, and then lightly knead to make a smooth dough.

3. Roll out biscuit dough on a flour-dusted surface. Stamp out biscuit characters using 7.5 cm (3 inch) cutters.

4. Put biscuits on to lightly greased baking sheets and cook for 12-15 minutes until browned around the edges.

5. Gently loosen biscuits with a palette knife and leave to cool on baking sheets.

Vanilla biscuits

Follow recipe for chocolate biscuits, above, but omit the cocoa at step 1 and add 15 g (½ oz) extra self-raising flour instead and a few drops of vanilla essence. Continue as chocolate biscuits, above.

To decorate

6. Sift icing sugar into a bowl. Stir in the water and mix to a thick paste. Divide icing between four small bowls and colour each one with a different food colouring.

7. Spoon a little pink icing into a greaseproof-paper piping bag. Snip off the tip and pipe icing on to ten biscuits to represent clothes, adding cake decorations as shown. Continue to ice remaining biscuits using blue, yellow and green icings.

8. Leave the icing to harden before serving biscuits.

Below: Chocolate & Vanilla Biscuits

· CHAPTER 3 ·

T·W·O-W·A·Y
S·T·R·E·T·C·H

If preparing meals for your child seems hard work at times, try these delicious meals that you can make for both yourself and your child in half the time. They're specially adapted to allow for children's less sophisticated tastes, without the grown-ups having to sacrifice any flavour.

SPICED LAMB WITH ORANGE

SERVES: 2 adults and 2 children

1 onion, sliced
300 ml (½ pint) orange juice
2 bay leaves
2 tbsp marmalade
2 tbsp white wine vinegar
½ tsp coriander seeds, crushed
½ tsp cumin seeds, crushed
½ shoulder of lamb, boned
salt and freshly ground black pepper
To serve:
6 large new potatoes, scrubbed
50 g (2 oz) mixed salad leaves
2 tbsp olive oil
2 tsp lemon juice
1 clove garlic, crushed
1 avocado
1 tomato, diced
2.5 cm (1 inch) piece cucumber, diced
butter

PREPARATION: 20 minutes
(plus 3-4 hours marinating)
COOKING: 1¼ hours

1. Put onion into a shallow dish or plastic container, large enough to take the lamb joint. Add orange juice, bay leaves, marmalade, vinegar and spices, and mix together well.

P·R·A·C·T·I·C·A·L·I·T·I·E·S

• Marinating meat before cooking adds flavour and tenderizes meat. Don't cover dish with foil; use clingfilm or a plastic bag instead.

2. Add lamb to the marinade, season well then cover with clingfilm and marinate in the fridge for 3-4 hours or overnight, turning lamb once.
3. Preheat the oven to 200°C, 400°F, Gas 6. Lift lamb out of marinade and tie into a neat shape with string. Place on a rack in a small roasting tin and pour a little water into the base.
4. Prick potatoes and put on a piece of foil or a small baking sheet. Cook lamb and potatoes on central oven shelf for 1¼ hours, or until juices run clear when a skewer is inserted into the thickest part of the lamb. Alternatively, bake lamb for 55 minutes then barbecue for 10 minutes each side.
5. Meanwhile, tear salad leaves into bite-sized pieces for adults' salad. Mix oil, lemon juice, garlic and seasoning in a bowl. Just before serving add salad leaves and toss.
6. Halve, peel and slice avocado, then chop a couple of slices and mix together with the tomato and cucumber. Spoon on to children's plates. Add the remaining avocado slices to adults' salad.
7. Carve lamb into thick slices. Chop a little for the children and arrange on their plates with a split and buttered potato. Cool slightly before serving. Serve lamb slices with salad and remaining potatoes, split and buttered for adults.

SPANISH TORTILLA

SERVES: 2 adults and 2-3 children

225 g (8 oz) potatoes, peeled and diced
1 tbsp oil
1 small onion, finely chopped
½ red pepper, deseeded and diced
3 tbsp frozen peas
4 eggs
1 tbsp milk
salt and freshly ground black pepper
15 g (½ oz) butter
To serve:
4 tomatoes
5 cm (2 inch) piece cucumber
few leaves Lollo Rosso lettuce
½ small onion, thinly sliced
3 tbsp olive oil
1 tbsp lemon juice
8 black olives, optional

PREPARATION: 15 minutes
COOKING: 20 minutes

1. Cook diced potatoes in lightly salted boiling water for 3-4 minutes until just tender. Drain, rinse with cold water and drain again.
2. Heat oil in an 18 cm (7 inch) frying pan. Add potatoes, onion, pepper and peas, and cook for 3-5 minutes, stirring occasionally until vegetables are lightly browned.
3. Beat together eggs, milk and seasoning. Add butter to pan and melt, then pour in egg mixture. Cook gently, without stirring, until set and

the underside of the tortilla turns a golden brown colour.
4. Transfer to a preheated grill and brown the top of the tortilla. Leave to stand for a few minutes while you make the salad.
5. Cut one tomato into small wedges and cucumber into chunky sticks; arrange on children's plates. Slice remaining tomatoes. Tear lettuce into bite-sized pieces and toss with onion.
6. Put olive oil, lemon juice and seasoning into a bowl. Whisk together then add salad

Above: Spanish Tortilla
Left: Spiced Lamb with Orange

ingredients and olives, if using. Toss together and arrange on adults' plates.
7. Cut the tortilla into large wedges for the adults and thin fingers for the children. Serve the tortilla warm with salad for adults.

PRAWN & ASPARAGUS QUICHE

SERVES: 4-6 adults and 2 children

Pastry:

225 g (8 oz) plain flour

pinch of salt

100 g (4 oz) butter or
*   margarine*

3 tbsp water

Filling:

150 g (6 oz) Cheddar cheese,
*   grated*

340 g (12½ oz) can asparagus
*   spears, drained*

100 g (4 oz) frozen prawns,
*   thawed*

3 eggs

150 ml (¼ pint) single cream

150 ml (¼ pint) milk

salt and freshly ground black
*   pepper*

To serve:

225 g (8 oz) baby new
*   potatoes, scrubbed*

carrot sticks

4 Little Gem lettuce leaves

mixed salad

PREPARATION: 40 minutes
COOKING: 50 minutes for large
quiche; 20-25 minutes for mini
quiches

1. Sift flour into a large bowl.
Add pinch of salt and butter
or margarine, cut into pieces.
Rub in with fingertips until
mixture resembles fine crumbs.

2. Add water and mix to a
smooth dough. Knead lightly
and roll out the dough on a
floured surface.

3. Use pastry to line a 23 cm
(9 inch) flan tin. Trim edge
and re-roll trimmings. Cut out
four circles of pastry with a
7.5 cm (3 inch) fluted pastry
cutter. Press into four sections
of a bun tray.

4. Chill for 15 minutes.
Preheat the oven to 200°C,
400°F, Gas 6.

5. Reserve a little grated
cheese and divide the
remainder between large and
small quiches. Drain asparagus
and arrange in large quiche.
Rinse prawns with cold water,
drain well and sprinkle
between asparagus.

6. Put eggs, cream, milk and
seasoning into a jug, whisk
and pour over quiches.

Sprinkle with reserved cheese.

7. Cook large quiche on centre
shelf of oven for 50 minutes
and mini quiches on the shelf
above for 20-25 minutes until
golden brown and well set.

8. Meanwhile, cook potatoes
in lightly salted boiling water
for 20 minutes.

9. Cool a few potatoes, dice,
and serve with mini quiches,
carrot sticks and lettuce leaves
for the children. Cut the large
quiche into wedges for the
adults and serve hot or cold
with drained potatoes and
mixed salad.

Below: Mini Prawn & Asparagus
Quiches served with diced
potatoes, carrot sticks and lettuce

SALMON & COD KEBABS

SERVES: 2 adults and 2 children

225 g (8 oz) cod fillet
2 salmon cutlets
2 cm (¾ inch) piece root
   ginger, peeled and finely
   chopped
2 tbsp oil
1 tbsp light soy sauce
Cucumber salad:
½ small cucumber
3 sticks celery
6 radishes
1 tbsp fresh chopped
   coriander
1 tsp vinegar
¼ tsp caster sugar
salt and freshly ground black
   pepper
To serve:
100 g (4 oz) basmati rice

PREPARATION: 30 minutes
(plus 2-3 hours marinating)
COOKING: 20 minutes

1. Skin cod fillet and cut flesh into chunks.
2. Halve each salmon cutlet by cutting around central bone. Remove skin and any small bones. Cut fish into chunks.
3. Mix chopped ginger, oil and soy sauce together in a shallow dish or plastic container.
4. Reserve a little of the fish for children's portions, cover and chill in the fridge. Toss the remaining fish in the ginger marinade, cover with clingfilm and leave to marinate for 2-3 hours.

5. Soak five wooden satay sticks in water for 20-30 minutes.
6. Cut one-quarter of the cucumber and 1 stick of celery into fingers for the children. Slice and quarter remaining cucumber, slice celery and cut radishes into wedges. Mix together in a bowl. Add coriander, vinegar, sugar and seasoning. Toss.
7. Cook rice in a saucepan of lightly salted boiling water for 8-10 minutes until just tender.
8. Thread the marinated fish

Above: Salmon & Cod Kebabs served with plain rice, cucumber and celery sticks

pieces on to four skewers. Thread the plain reserved fish on to remaining skewer. Cook under a hot grill or barbecue for 8-10 minutes.
9. Spoon rice on to plates. Add marinated kebabs and cucumber salad to adult servings. For children, take fish off skewer and cut up. Cool slightly before serving with cucumber and celery sticks.

T·W·O·-W·A·Y S·T·R·E·T·C·H

FISHY DINNER

MAKES: 2 adult portions and
2 baby portions

Base, and for baby:
325 g (12 oz) haddock
*1 carrot, peeled and finely
  chopped*
2 tbsp long-grain rice
6 tbsp milk
*75 g (3 oz) spinach leaves,
  thoroughly washed and
  shredded*
2 tsp Marmite
...and for the adults:
grated rind of 1 lemon
50 g (2 oz) butter
*salt and freshly ground black
  pepper*
*200 g (7 oz) packet frozen
  puff pastry, just thawed*
1 egg, beaten
To serve:
*potatoes tossed in butter and
  parsley*
steamed carrots and leeks

PREPARATION: 1 hour
COOKING: 40 minutes

1. Preheat the oven to 220°C,
425°F, Gas 7. To make base,
cut off two 125 g (5 oz) pieces
of haddock – the rest is for
your baby's portions.
2. Put all of the fish, carrot,
rice and milk in a saucepan.
Cover and cook for 8-10 minutes, or until fish flakes when
pressed with a knife and rice
is tender.
3. Place spinach in a steamer
over fish or use a colander and
cover with a saucepan lid.

Cook for the last 5 minutes of
fish cooking time.
4. Lift out fish with a slotted
spoon or fish slice, set aside.
5. For the baby portions, skin
small pieces of fish, flake
using a knife and fork, being
careful to remove any bones.
6. Process, liquidize or mash
fish with carrot, rice and milk
mixture plus 3 tbsp of spinach
adding a little extra milk if it
is too thick.
7. Spoon into sterilized
individual ramekins or sections
of an ice-cube tray. Cover and
store in fridge or freezer until
required. Reheat thoroughly.
8. For adult portions, beat the
lemon rind, butter and
seasoning together.
9. Roll pastry out thinly on a

lightly floured surface to a
30 cm (12 inch) square. Cut
two 15 x 20 cm (6 x 8 inch)
rectangles.
10. Put one-quarter of the
remaining spinach into centre
of pastry rectangles, season.
Skin fish, spread one side with
lemon butter, then put butter-
side down on to spinach.
11. Spread fish with the
remaining butter and top with
remaining spinach.
12. Brush the pastry edges
with beaten egg. Fold up like

P·R·A·C·T·I·C·A·L·I·T·I·E·S

• Always store fresh fish in the
  fridge until needed and cook
  it the same day it is bought.
• If using frozen fish, defrost
  thoroughly in the fridge first.

a parcel, squeezing the edges together tightly.

13. Put pastry join side down on to a lightly greased baking sheet. Brush with beaten egg and decorate with fish shapes cut from remaining pastry.

14. To make pastry twists for baby portions, spread remaining pastry with Marmite, then beaten egg. Cut 15 cm (6 inch) long strips, twist like a corkscrew and put on a greased baking sheet, pressing ends down firmly.

15. Cook the pies for 25-30 minutes and the twists for 8-10 minutes.

16. Serve twists warm or cold with baby portions of fish. Serve adult pies with potatoes tossed in butter and parsley, and steamed carrots and leeks.

Below: Lamb Hotpot
Left: Fishy Dinner

LAMB HOTPOT

MAKES: 2 adult portions and 2 baby portions

Base, and for baby:
675 g (1½ lb) neck of lamb
1 onion, chopped
½ medium-sized swede, diced
1 turnip or kohlrabi, diced
2 sprigs rosemary
450 ml (¾ pint) hot beef stock
...and for the adults:
450 g (1 lb) potatoes,
*   scrubbed and sliced*
75 g (3 oz) black pudding
1 dessert apple, peeled, cored
*   and sliced*
salt and freshly ground black
*   pepper*
25 g (1 oz) butter
To serve:
75 g (3 oz) green beans,
*   trimmed*

PREPARATION: 35 minutes
COOKING: 2¼ hours

1. Preheat the oven to 180°C, 350°F, Gas 4. To make the base, put lamb into a 1.75 litre (3½ pint) casserole dish. Add onion, swede and turnip or kohlrabi to casserole dish with rosemary and stock. Cover and cook for 1½ hours.

2. Meanwhile, for adult portions cook potato slices in lightly salted boiling water for 5 minutes until just tender. Drain and rinse with cold water. Drain again.

3. Remove skin from black pudding and slice.

4. Remove two pieces of meat from casserole and cut meat off the bone, discarding any fat. Process or liquidize with 6 tbsp of the vegetables, adding a little stock if required. Spoon into sterilized individual ramekins or sections of an ice-cube tray. Cover, store in fridge or freezer until required.

5. Reserve a few slices of apple for baby and add remainder to casserole with black pudding and seasoning. Arrange the potato slices in an overlapping pattern over top of casserole and then season and dot with a little butter.

6. Cook hotpot at 200°C, 400°F, Gas 6, for 45 minutes until potatoes are browned. Steam beans for 10 minutes until just tender and serve with hotpot. Reheat the baby portions thoroughly and serve with reserved apple slices and a few green beans.

TWO-WAY STRETCH

PORK & APPLE STRUDEL

SERVES: 4 adults and 2 children

450 g (1 lb) pork and herb
sausages
1 small onion, finely chopped
1 dessert apple, peeled, cored
and chopped
100 g (4 oz) button
mushrooms, chopped
salt and freshly ground black
pepper
50 g (2 oz) butter
1 tbsp oil
270 g (10 oz) packet frozen
filo pastry, just thawed
Bean salad:
75 g (3 oz) green beans,
trimmed
2 tbsp olive oil
1 tsp vinegar
½ tsp coarse grain mustard
100 g (4 oz) frozen
sweetcorn, thawed, or half
198 g (7 oz) can
sweetcorn, drained
213 g (7½ oz) can red kidney
beans, drained
1 tbsp fresh chopped parsley
1 stick celery

PREPARATION: 40 minutes
COOKING: 20 minutes

1. Preheat the oven to 220°C,
425°F, Gas 7.
2. Slit the sausages lengthways
and remove skin. Mix together
sausagemeat, onion, apple,
mushrooms and seasoning.
3. Melt butter in a small
saucepan, add oil.
4. Unroll pastry. Place one

sheet of pastry in front of you
so the shortest side is nearest
you. Divide sausagemeat
mixture into five and shape
one portion into a sausage
shape along bottom edge of
pastry, leaving a little pastry
uncovered at each end of the
sausagemeat.
5. Roll pastry up around the
sausagemeat and continue
rolling until you reach the
centre. Brush remaining
portion of pastry lightly with
butter and oil, then roll to
end. Squeeze pastry ends
together to seal. Put on
greased baking sheet.
6. Repeat, using four of the
remaining pastry sheets in the
same way.
7. Brush top of strudels with
butter mixture. Tear
remaining pastry sheet into
strips and twist over strudels.
Brush with butter again.
8. Cook for 20 minutes until
pastry is golden brown.
9. Meanwhile, make the bean
salad. Cut the green beans
into 2.5 cm (1 inch) lengths.
Cook in a saucepan of lightly
salted boiling water for
2 minutes. Drain, rinse
thoroughly with cold water
and drain again.
10. Mix oil, vinegar, mustard
and seasoning together in a
salad bowl. Reserve some
green beans and sweetcorn for
the children, then add the
remainder to the dressing with
red kidney beans and chopped

parsley. Slice celery, add to
bean salad and toss well.
11. Cut each strudel in half
and serve with the bean salad
for adults. Cut into small
slices for children and serve,
slightly cooled, with plain
green beans and sweetcorn.

CHEESE & VEGETABLE STRUDEL

SERVES: 5 adults and 2 children

50 g (2 oz) margarine
50 g (2 oz) plain flour
450 ml (¾ pint) milk
salt and freshly ground black
pepper
150 g (6 oz) Red Leicester
cheese
100 g (4 oz) broccoli
325 g (12 oz) potatoes,
peeled and diced
200 g (7 oz) frozen
sweetcorn, thawed, or
198 g (7 oz) can
sweetcorn, drained
75 g (3 oz) butter
1 tbsp oil
270 g (10 oz) packet frozen
filo pastry, just thawed
1 small onion, finely chopped
1 tbsp sesame seeds
¼ tsp paprika
To serve:
Bean salad as recipe, left

PREPARATION: 45 minutes
COOKING: 20 minutes

1. Preheat the oven to 220°C,
425°F, Gas 7. Melt the
margarine in a small saucepan.

Stir in the flour then gradually whisk in milk. Bring to the boil whisking continuously until the mixture has thickened and become smooth. Season to taste.

2. Grate half the cheese and dice remainder. Stir grated cheese into sauce until melted.

3. Cut broccoli into florets and dice the stalks.

4. Cook potatoes in lightly salted boiling water for 3 minutes. Add broccoli 1 minute from end of cooking time. Drain the vegetables, rinse with cold water and drain again thoroughly.

5. Stir diced cheese, potatoes, broccoli and sweetcorn into the sauce.

6. Melt butter in a small saucepan, add oil.

7. Divide vegetable mixture into six. Follow steps 4 and 5 of Pork & Apple Strudel recipe (see page 48), to make children's portions using one sheet of pastry, one portion of filling and a little of the melted butter and oil mixture.

8. Add chopped onion to remaining vegetable mixture. Make five adult strudels with

Above: Cheese & Vegetable Strudel and Pork & Apple Strudel served with green beans, sweetcorn and bean salad

remaining pastry and filling as shown above.

9. Brush all the strudels with butter and oil, sprinkle with sesame seeds and paprika. Cook for 20 minutes until strudels are golden brown. Serve with bean salad for the adults and plain green beans and sweetcorn for the children, as steps 9 to 11 of the Pork & Apple Strudel recipe.

VEGETABLE LASAGNE

MAKES: 2 adult portions and 2 baby portions

Base, and for baby:
1 small fennel bulb
2 tbsp + 1 tsp olive oil
1 small onion, finely
*   chopped*
2 carrots, peeled and diced
325 g (12 oz) potato,
*   scrubbed and diced*
½ red pepper, deseeded and
*   diced*
100 g (4 oz) button
*   mushrooms, sliced*
397 g (14 oz) can tomatoes
½ tsp sugar
4 sheets dried lasagne
2-3 tbsp milk

...and for the adults:
1 clove garlic, crushed
salt and freshly ground black
*   pepper*
25 g (1 oz) butter
25 g (1 oz) plain flour
300 ml (½ pint) milk
75 g (3 oz) Cheddar cheese,
*   grated*

To serve:
bread sticks
mixed leaf salad
herb or garlic bread

PREPARATION: 50 minutes
COOKING: 45 minutes

1. Preheat the oven to 200°C, 400°F, Gas 6. For the base, halve fennel and cut out woody core, then chop into small pieces.
2. Heat 2 tbsp oil in a
saucepan and fry the onion, carrot and potato for 5 minutes, stirring occasionally, until they are softened but not browned.
3. Add fennel, pepper and mushrooms and cook for 3 minutes, stirring occasionally. Stir in the tomatoes and sugar, bring to the boil, then cover and simmer for 10 minutes until the mixture thickens.
4. Meanwhile, bring a saucepan of water to the boil, add 1 tsp of oil, then the sheets of lasagne, one at a time. Cook the lasagne according to packet instructions until it becomes quite tender.
5. Drain pasta, rinse with cold water and drain again.
6. For baby portions, process, liquidize or mash 6 tbsp of tomato mixture with 2-3 tbsp milk and set aside. For adult portions, stir in garlic and seasoning to taste.
7. To make the white sauce for adult portions, heat butter in a saucepan, stir in flour and cook for 1 minute. Gradually add milk and bring to the boil, stirring until thickened and smooth. Season well.
8. Spoon half of the tomato mixture into the base of a 1 litre (2 pint) ovenproof dish. Cover with two sheets of pasta and the rest of the tomato mixture.
9. Spoon half the white sauce over the dish. Reserve 2 tsp grated cheese and sprinkle half of the remainder over the
white sauce. Cover with two sheets of pasta, trimming to fit the shape of the dish. Reserve the pasta trimmings to use for the baby portions.
10. Spoon the remaining sauce over dish and sprinkle with remaining grated cheese.
11. Complete baby portions by finely chopping pasta trimmings and stirring 4 tsp into reserved tomato and milk mixture with 2 tsp reserved grated cheese. Spoon into sterilized individual ramekins or sections of an ice-cube tray. Cover and store in fridge or freezer until required. Reheat thoroughly and serve with bread sticks.
12. To complete the lasagne, cook for 35 minutes until golden brown. Serve with a mixed leaf salad and herb or garlic bread.

P·R·A·C·T·I·C·A·L·I·T·I·E·S

- Reheat food thoroughly, making sure it is really hot all the way through. Stir foods well so that there are no hot spots – especially important if you are using a microwave.
- To speed up reheating, make mixtures thick, and then thin with formula, or cows' milk if for babies over 1 year of age.
- Adjust cooking times if using fresh lasagne – it needs about half the time of dried; or use pre-cooked lasagne to save time.

Right: Vegetable Lasagne served with bread sticks, a mixed leaf salad and herb bread

T·W·O·-·W·A·Y S·T·R·E·T·C·H

CHICKEN BREAST STIR-FRY WITH EGG-FRIED RICE

MAKES: 2 adult portions and 2 baby portions

Base, and for baby:
3 carrots, peeled
3 sticks celery, trimmed
2 courgettes, trimmed
1 leek, washed
2 x 150 g (6 oz) chicken
*   breasts, diced*
3-5 tbsp milk
...and for the adults:
2 tbsp yellow bean paste
2 tbsp light soy sauce
2 tbsp dry vermouth or dry
*   sherry*
2 tsp tomato purée
100 g (4 oz) long-grain rice
1 tbsp oil
25 g (1 oz) blanched almonds
3 spring onions, trimmed and
*   thinly sliced*
1 egg, beaten
freshly ground black pepper

PREPARATION: 40 minutes
COOKING: 20 minutes

1. To make the base, cut carrots in half lengthways and then cut one-quarter into thin matchstick strips, and put to one side. Cut the remaining carrot, along with the celery, courgettes and leek, into diagonal slices.
2. For baby portions, put one-quarter of the chicken in a small saucepan with 75 g (3 oz) of the sliced vegetables and 3 tbsp milk. Cover and

simmer for 10 minutes until chicken is thoroughly cooked.
3. Process, liquidize or mash chicken and vegetable mixture, adding a little extra milk if required. Spoon into sterilized individual ramekins or sections of an ice-cube tray. Cover and store in fridge or freezer until required. Reheat the mixture thoroughly and serve with some of the prepared carrot matchsticks.
4. For adult portions, put the yellow bean paste, soy sauce, dry vermouth or sherry and tomato purée in a bowl and mix them together well. Add the remaining chicken and toss in soy sauce mixture.
5. Boil rice in lightly salted water for 8-10 minutes until just tender. Drain, rinse and drain again. Set rice, chicken and vegetables aside until they are required.
6. Heat oil in a non-stick frying pan and fry almonds

Above: Chicken Breast Stir-fry served with Egg-fried Rice and carrot sticks

until lightly browned.
7. Add chicken, lifting out of soy mixture with a slotted spoon. Cook for 5 minutes, stirring fairly frequently, until the chicken is browned.
8. Reserve 1 tbsp of spring onions for rice garnish and add remaining onions and vegetables to chicken. Cook for 5 minutes, stirring frequently until tender.
9. Stir in the remaining soy sauce mixture and cook for 1 minute. Then spoon into a serving dish.
10. Mix egg and plenty of black pepper into hot, drained rice (reheat if necessary) and stir, over the heat, until egg has lightly scrambled. Then spoon into a serving dish and sprinkle with reserved spring onion slices.

HERBY ROAST CHICKEN

SERVES: 3 adults and 2 children

1 lemon
100 g (4 oz) medium-fat soft
*   cheese*
25 g (1 oz) butter, at room
*   temperature*
1 tbsp fresh chopped parsley
1 tbsp fresh chopped tarragon
salt and freshly ground black
*   pepper*
1.7 kg (3¾ lb) fresh chicken,
*   without giblets*
To serve:
225 g (8 oz) baby new
*   potatoes, scrubbed and*
*   halved*
4 carrots, sliced
2 courgettes, sliced
115 g (4½ oz) baby corn,
*   halved lengthways*
2 tbsp olive oil
1 tsp grated lemon rind
2 tsp lemon juice
To garnish:
sprigs of flat-leafed parsley
lemon slices, halved

PREPARATION: 40 minutes
COOKING: 1½ hours

1. Preheat the oven to 190°C,
375°F, Gas 5. Grate rind
from half the lemon. Cut
lemon in half and squeeze
juice from the grated half;
slice the remainder.
2. Put the lemon rind and
juice, soft cheese, butter, herbs
and seasoning into a bowl and
beat together until smooth.
3. Rinse chicken inside and

out with cold water; drain
well. Put on a chopping board.
Insert a small knife into top of
chicken breast to loosen the
skin. Slide finger under skin
and loosen it from both sides
of the breast.
4. Spoon herb mixture under
the skin and ease evenly over
both sides of breast.
5. Put chicken in a roasting
tin, arrange lemon slices over
the centre of breast and cover
loosely with foil.
6. Cook for 1 hour. Remove
foil and continue cooking for a
further 30 minutes until
chicken is well browned. To
test, insert a skewer into the
thickest part of the leg and
breast; if juices run clear,
chicken is cooked. If not, cook
for a further 15 minutes and
then retest.
7. Meanwhile cook new
potatoes in a saucepan of

lightly salted boiling water for
last 20 minutes of chicken's
cooking time.
8. Add carrots to potatoes
halfway through cooking time;
add the courgettes for last
5 minutes and corn for last
2 minutes.
9. Drain the vegetables. Chop
some for the children and
leave to cool slightly. Mix
olive oil, lemon rind, juice and
seasoning in vegetable pan.
Toss the remaining vegetables
in the dressing.
10. Transfer the chicken to a
serving plate and garnish with
parsley and the halved lemon
slices. Serve herby chicken
with lemon vegetables for
adults and with plain
vegetables for children.

Below: Herby Roast Chicken
served with mixed vegetables

· CHAPTER 4 ·

M·E·A·T·L·E·S·S

M·E·A·L·S

Increasingly, many families are becoming totally vegetarian or simply try to cut down on the amount of red meat they eat. The following recipes offer tasty meat-free meals that don't take hours to prepare, and still provide all the healthy goodness you and your children need in your diet.

GOLDEN PEANUT BURGERS

MAKES: 8

1 tbsp oil
1 small onion, finely chopped
425 g (15 oz) can cannellini
   beans, drained
100 g (4 oz) breadcrumbs
4 tbsp crunchy peanut butter
1 tsp mild chilli powder,
   optional
1 tsp lemon juice
salt and freshly ground black
   pepper
1 egg, beaten
100 g (4 oz) porridge oats
oil for frying
To serve:
8 sesame seed baps
salad garnish

PREPARATION: 15 minutes
COOKING: 8 minutes

1. Heat oil in a small saucepan and gently fry onion until soft.
2. Mash beans roughly with a fork. Mix with the onion, breadcrumbs, peanut butter, chilli powder, if using, lemon juice and seasoning.
3. Divide mixture into eight, shape into burgers.
4. Pour beaten egg on to a plate. Dip burgers in egg then toss in oats until evenly coated.
5. Heat a little oil in a large frying pan. Gently fry burgers for about 4 minutes on each side or until golden. Serve in baps with salad garnish.

Left: Golden Peanut Burgers

CHEESY PANCAKE BAKE

SERVES: 4

Pancake:
50 g (2 oz) plain flour
50 g (2 oz) wholemeal flour
pinch of salt
2 eggs
200 ml (⅓ pint) milk mixed
    with 45 ml (3 tbsp) water
oil for frying
Filling:
50 g (2 oz) butter
275 g (10 oz) packet frozen
    spinach, thawed
225 g (8 oz) mushrooms,
    sliced
¼ tsp grated nutmeg
freshly ground black pepper
Sauce:
25 g (1 oz) butter
25 g (1 oz) plain flour
450 ml (¾ pint) milk
salt and freshly ground black
    pepper
75 g (3 oz) Cheddar cheese,
    grated
25 g (1 oz) breadcrumbs

PREPARATION: 30 minutes
COOKING: 35 minutes

1. Preheat the oven to 375°F, 190°C, Gas 5. To make pancakes, mix the flours and salt. Add eggs, beat until smooth then gradually add milk and water.

2. Heat a little oil in an 18 cm (7 inch) frying pan. When it is very hot, pour in just enough batter to coat the base. Cook until golden brown under-neath, then turn over and cook the other side. Make eight pancakes and put to one side.

3. Melt 25 g (1 oz) butter in a frying pan and very gently cook the spinach for 8 minutes. Fry the mushrooms for 5 minutes in the remaining butter. Mix well with the spinach and season with the nutmeg and black pepper.

4. Divide the spinach mixture between the pancakes and fold into quarters. Arrange them in a shallow ovenproof dish.

5. To make the sauce, melt the butter in a small saucepan and stir in the flour. Cook gently for about 1 minute then gradually add the milk, stirring continuously until the sauce thickens and comes to the boil. Season.

6. Add 50 g (2 oz) of grated cheese to the sauce. Pour the sauce evenly over the pancakes and sprinkle the top with the remaining grated cheese and the breadcrumbs.

7. Place in the oven and bake for about 35 minutes until the topping is golden brown.

Above: Cheesy Pancake Bake

P·R·A·C·T·I·C·A·L·I·T·I·E·S

• If your family aren't fond of spinach, use sweetcorn in the Cheesy Pancake Bake.
• You can make these dishes ahead and freeze or refrigerate before cooking.

M·E·A·T·L·E·S·S M·E·A·L·S

FISH & CHIP PIE

SERVES: 4

25 g (1 oz) butter
1 small onion, finely chopped
25 g (1 oz) flour
300 ml (½ pint) milk
2 tomatoes, skinned and
    quartered
1 tsp capers, chopped
100 g (4 oz) frozen peas
salt and freshly ground black
    pepper
450 g (1 lb) cod fillets
675 g (1½ lb) potatoes, peeled
2 tbsp oil
1 tbsp lemon juice

PREPARATION: 30 minutes
COOKING: 35 minutes

1. Preheat the oven to 200°C, 400°F, Gas 6. Gently melt the butter in a medium-sized saucepan and fry the onion until softened. Add the flour and cook for 1 further minute. Gradually add the milk, stirring continuously until the

Below: Fish & Chip Pie

sauce thickens and comes to the boil. Add the tomatoes, capers, peas and seasoning.
2. Skin the cod fillets and cut into chunks. Stir into the sauce.
3. Turn into shallow oven-proof dish or four small dishes.
4. Cut potatoes into matchstick-sized chips. Place in a saucepan and pour over boiling water. Bring back to the boil and cook for 2 minutes. Drain. Stir in the oil and lemon juice and season.
5. Spoon over the fish mixture. Bake for about 35 minutes until golden.

TOPPING SPUDS

SERVES: 4

1. Choose four large baking potatoes, wash and bake in centre of oven 190°C, 375°F, Gas 5, for 1-1½ hours.
2. Cut a cross in top of each potato and spoon in topping.

TANGY TUNA & ONION

200 g (7 oz) can tuna,
    drained
4 tbsp mayonnaise
1 tbsp tomato
    ketchup
dash Worcester
    sauce
4 spring
    onions,
    trimmed
    and sliced

PREPARATION: 5 minutes

1. Mix the tuna with the mayonnaise, ketchup and Worcester sauce.
2. Add half of spring onions to mixture. Use to top each spud, sprinkle with rest of onion.

RANCH-STYLE BEANS

1 tbsp oil
½ green pepper, deseeded and
    diced
225 g (8 oz) can baked beans
225 g (8 oz) can red kidney
    beans, drained and rinsed
1 tbsp tomato or barbecue
    relish

PREPARATION AND
COOKING: 10 minutes

1. Heat oil in a small saucepan and fry the pepper until soft.
2. Add both the baked beans and the kidney beans, together with the relish, and heat through before serving.

FLORIDA FRUIT & NUT

225 g (8 oz) cottage cheese
2 tbsp mandarin segments
50 g (2 oz) peanuts and
    raisins

PREPARATION: 5 minutes

1. Mix all the ingredients together and serve.

Right (from top): Tangy Tuna & Onion, Ranch-style Beans and Florida Fruit & Nut Topping Spuds

M·E·A·T·L·E·S·S M·E·A·L·S

PASTA WITH VEGETABLE BOLOGNAISE

SERVES: 4

100 g (4 oz) red lentils
1 tbsp oil
1 medium-sized onion,
chopped
1 clove garlic, crushed
225 g (8 oz) mushrooms,
sliced
2 carrots, peeled and diced
2 sticks celery, sliced
400 g (14 oz) can chopped
tomatoes
1 tbsp tomato purée
1 tsp dried mixed herbs
1 tsp Marmite
salt and freshly ground black
pepper
325 g (12 oz) pasta bows
Parmesan cheese, for
sprinkling, optional

PREPARATION: 20 minutes
COOKING: 20 minutes

1. Place the lentils in a large saucepan of cold water and bring to the boil. Skim the surface until it is clear and cook for 10 minutes. Drain.
2. Heat the oil in a large saucepan and gently fry the onion and garlic until soft.
3. Add mushrooms, carrots and celery to the saucepan along with the lentils, tomatoes, tomato purée, herbs, Marmite and seasoning. Cover and simmer for 20 minutes.
4. About 10 minutes before the sauce is ready, cook the pasta in lightly salted boiling water until just tender. Drain and serve with the sauce. Sprinkle with a little Parmesan cheese, if liked.

Below: Pasta with Vegetable
Bolognaise
Right top: Playtime Pizzas
Right bottom: Saucy Tuna
Animals

SAUCY TUNA ANIMALS

SERVES: 4

150 g (6 oz) broccoli, broken
into tiny florets
3 carrots, finely diced
225 g (8 oz) tricolour pasta
animals
1 tsp oil
40 g (1½ oz) margarine
40 g (1½ oz) plain flour
600 ml (1 pint) milk
150 g (6 oz) Cheddar cheese,
grated
198 g (7 oz) can tuna in
brine, drained
salt and freshly ground black
pepper

PREPARATION: 15 minutes
COOKING: 15 minutes

1. Bring a large saucepan of salted water to the boil. Add the vegetables, pasta and oil. Bring the water back to the boil and cook for 8 minutes until vegetables and pasta are tender. Drain well.
2. Meanwhile, heat margarine in a separate saucepan. Stir in flour and cook for 1 minute. Gradually stir in the milk and bring to the boil, stirring until thickened and smooth.
3. Stir 100 g (4 oz) of the grated cheese into the sauce. Flake tuna and stir into sauce with the pasta and vegetables. Season. Reheat gently.
4. Spoon on to warmed plates, sprinkle with the remaining cheese. Serve immediately.

PLAYTIME PIZZAS

SERVES: 4

4 tomatoes

25 g (1 oz) mushrooms, thinly sliced

4 spring onions, trimmed and roughly chopped

2 tbsp sweetcorn

½ tsp mixed herbs

salt and freshly ground black pepper

8 crumpets

75 g (3 oz) Cheddar or mozzarella cheese, grated

½ green pepper, optional

½ red pepper, optional

PREPARATION AND COOKING: 20 minutes

1. Place tomatoes in deep heat-proof bowl and pour boiling water over. Let stand for 1 minute, drain, peel and chop.

2. Add mushrooms to chopped tomatoes along with onions, sweetcorn and herbs. Season.

3. Heat grill, toast crumpets on both sides. Top each with a little tomato mixture.

4. Sprinkle the grated cheese over the crumpets. If liked, slice the red and green peppers and arrange on top of the pizzas in a noughts and crosses design. Grill until the cheese is bubbling and golden.

P·R·A·C·T·I·C·A·L·I·T·I·E·S

- If preferred, use muffins or bap rolls as an alternative to crumpet bases for the Playtime Pizzas.
- Pasta is always popular with all ages and makes a quick and easy meal. Look for the different pasta shapes and colours that are available in your supermarket.

M·E·A·T·L·E·S·S M·E·A·L·S

HADDOCK & PASTA GRATIN

SERVES: 4

150 g (6 oz) pasta shells
150 g (6 oz) broccoli
6 spring onions, trimmed and sliced
100 g (4 oz) frozen sweetcorn
450 g (1 lb) smoked haddock fillet
600 ml (1 pint) milk
50 g (2 oz) sunflower margarine
50 g (2 oz) plain flour
125 g (5 oz) Cheddar cheese, grated
salt and freshly ground black pepper
2 tbsp breadcrumbs

PREPARATION: 20 minutes
COOKING: 30 minutes

1. Cook pasta in a large pan of lightly salted boiling water for 10 minutes or until tender.
2. Meanwhile, cut the broccoli into small florets and slice the stalks.
3. Add broccoli to pasta 3 minutes before end of cooking time and spring onions and sweetcorn 1 minute before end of cooking time. Drain and keep hot.
4. Cut haddock into two or three pieces and place in a large saucepan with the milk. Cover, simmer for 8-10 minutes until fish flakes easily.
5. Lift fish out of pan with a fish slice. Peel off skin and break into flakes, discarding bones. Strain milk and reserve.

Below: Haddock & Pasta Gratin

6. Melt the margarine in a saucepan, stir in the flour then gradually add reserved milk. Bring to the boil, stirring continuously, until sauce is thickened and smooth.
7. Stir 100 g (4 oz) of cheese into the sauce and season. Fold in the pasta, vegetables and fish, and spoon into a shallow ovenproof dish.
8. Sprinkle with breadcrumbs and remaining cheese. Cook under a preheated grill for 8-10 minutes until golden and heated through. Serve.

CHEESY SHELLS

SERVES: 4

225 g (8 oz) wholewheat pasta shells
4 tsp oil
2 leeks
50 g (2 oz) butter
2 tsp pesto sauce
150 ml (¼ pint) single cream
75 g (3 oz) Sage Derby cheese, crumbled into small pieces
75 g (3 oz) Double Gloucester cheese, crumbled into small pieces
75 g (3 oz) White Cheshire cheese, crumbled into small pieces
salt and freshly ground black pepper

PREPARATION: 10 minutes
COOKING: 20 minutes

1. Bring a large saucepan of salted water to the boil. Add

PETITE PIZZAS

MAKES: 2

2 mini pitta breads
1 tbsp tomato relish or
  ketchup
2 tbsp frozen sweetcorn,
  thawed
4 tbsp grated Cheddar cheese
To serve:
coleslaw, cucumber sticks and
  apple wedges

PREPARATION: 5 minutes
COOKING: 5 minutes

1. Sprinkle pitta breads with a little water and cook under a preheated grill until just beginning to puff up.
2. Turn over and spread surface with tomato relish or ketchup. Sprinkle with sweetcorn, then top the pizzas with grated cheese.
3. Return to grill and cook until the cheese is bubbling. Cut into pieces and cool a little before serving.

pasta and 1 tsp oil. Bring water back to the boil and cook pasta for 8-10 minutes until tender.
2. Meanwhile, halve the leeks lengthways and wash thoroughly, then drain and thinly slice.
3. Drain pasta. Melt butter and remaining oil in drained pasta pan and fry leeks for 5 minutes until softened.
4. Mix pesto with the cream and add to the leeks, together with the pasta, cheeses and seasoning. Toss together and reheat gently. Spoon on to warmed serving plates. Serve immediately.

Above: Petite Pizza served with coleslaw, cucumber sticks and apple wedges
Below: Cheesy Shells

· C H A P T E R 5 ·

F·A·M·I·L·Y

M·E·A·L·S

If you want to feed your family fast, follow our plan-and freeze-ahead recipes. Make three different dishes from three basic ingredients: chicken, mince and cheese sauce. In between, we offer filling family meals you can leave to cook in the oven until you're ready to eat, plus three simple and speedy salads.

BASIC CHICKEN RECIPE

12 large chicken thighs
50 g (2 oz) butter
2 tbsp oil
3 onions, sliced
3 tbsp plain flour
600 ml (1 pint) chicken stock
salt and freshly ground black
 pepper

PREPARATION: 10 minutes
COOKING: 1¼ hours

1. Preheat the oven to 180°C, 350°F, Gas 4. Trim away the fat from the chicken thighs.

2. Heat butter and oil in a large frying pan and fry chicken portions in batches until browned on both sides.
3. Remove chicken with a slotted spoon and put in a large roasting tin.
4. Fry onion for 5 minutes until softened. Stir in flour. Add stock and seasoning and bring to the boil, stirring to prevent flour forming lumps.
5. Pour mixture over chicken. Cover tightly with foil or a lid and cook for 1 hour until chicken is thoroughly cooked.
6. Drain chicken and set aside.

Measure out stock and onion mixture into three equal amounts. Reserve chicken pieces for use in the following recipes (use four per dish).

CHICKEN PEPPERONATA

SERVES: 4

½ *red pepper, deseeded and cut into thin strips*
½ *yellow pepper, deseeded and cut into thin strips*
225 g (8 oz) can tomatoes, drained and roughly chopped
⅓ *Basic Chicken Recipe, prepared as above left*
To serve:
boiled baby new potatoes
steamed runner beans

PREPARATION: 15 minutes
REHEATING: 15 minutes

1. Cook strips of pepper in lightly salted boiling water for 1 minute. Drain, rinse with cold water and drain again.
2. Stir tomatoes into chicken stock mixture together with blanched peppers. Let cool.
To freeze: divide chicken thighs and pepper mixture into four portions and put into freezer bags. Seal and label. Freeze for up to 3 months.
To defrost: thaw for 6 hours or use a microwave.

Far left: Chicken Pepperonata
Left: Creamed Chicken with Coriander served with brown rice

To reheat: bring to boil in a saucepan, cover, cook for 15 minutes, stirring occasionally, or use a microwave.
Serve with new potatoes and steamed runner beans.

CREAMED CHICKEN WITH CORIANDER

SERVES: 4

50 g (2 oz) creamed coconut, crumbled
grated rind and juice of ½ orange
1 tbsp fresh chopped coriander
⅓ *Basic Chicken Recipe, prepared as above left*
To serve:
easy-cook brown rice

PREPARATION: 10 minutes
REHEATING: 15 minutes

1. Add the coconut, orange rind, orange juice and coriander to the chicken stock mixture. Stir well until the coconut has melted.
2. Allow to cool thoroughly.
To freeze: divide chicken thighs and coconut mixture into four portions and put into freezer bags. Seal and label. Freeze for up to 3 months.
To defrost: thaw for 6 hours or use a microwave.
To reheat: bring to boil in a saucepan and cook for 15 minutes, stirring occasionally, or use a microwave. Serve with easy-cook brown rice.

SOMERSET CHICKEN

SERVES: 4

2 tbsp olive oil

4 large chicken thighs

1 onion, sliced

3 rashers smoked back bacon,
    derinded and chopped

100 g (4 oz) button
    mushrooms, halved

2 tbsp plain flour

300 ml (½ pint) dry cider

1 chicken stock cube

1 tbsp fresh chopped sage or
    ¼ tsp dried

salt and freshly ground black
    pepper

325 g (12 oz) carrots, peeled
    and diced

325 g (12 oz) swede, peeled
    and diced

25 g (1 oz) butter

3 tbsp water

fresh chopped sage or chopped
    parsley to garnish

PREPARATION: 30 minutes
COOKING: 1½-2 hours

1. Preheat the oven to 160° C,
325° F, Gas 3. Heat oil in a
flameproof casserole dish or
frying pan. Fry chicken on
both sides until browned.
Drain and transfer to a plate if
using a flameproof dish, or an
ovenproof casserole if using a
frying pan.
2. Fry onion and bacon for
5 minutes. Add mushrooms
and cook for 2 minutes.
3. Sprinkle flour over, stir and
cook for 1 minute. Add cider,

stock cube, sage and seasoning
and bring to boil. Return
chicken to flameproof casserole
dish or pour mixture over
chicken if using ovenproof
casserole dish.
4. Cover and cook for 1½-2
hours or until juices run clear.
5. Cook carrots and swede in a
saucepan of boiling water for
3 minutes. Drain and transfer
to an ovenproof casserole dish.
6. Add butter, water and
seasoning. Cook on same shelf
as chicken for 1½-2 hours.
7. Sprinkle chicken with sage
or parsley and serve.

Below: Somerset Chicken

CHICKEN & BACON PIES

SERVES: 4

⅓ Basic Chicken Recipe,
    prepared as on page 62

4 rashers streaky bacon,
    derinded and chopped

1 tbsp oil

100 g (4 oz) button
    mushrooms, quartered

50 g (2 oz) stoned prunes,
    chopped

454 g (1 lb) packet puff
    pastry, chilled

To serve:

steamed courgettes, carrots
    and sugar peas

PREPARATION: 35 minutes
REHEATING: 25 minutes

1. Remove the skin and bone from the four chicken thighs and chop meat. Divide evenly between four individual oven/freezerproof dishes.

2. Fry bacon in the oil until golden. Drain, and divide between dishes.

3. Add the mushrooms to the pan and cook for 3 minutes. Drain, and divide between the four dishes.

4. Add the chopped prunes to dishes, then pour the stock and onion mixture over chicken. Allow to cool thoroughly.

5. Thinly roll out the puff pastry on a lightly floured surface and cut out pastry lids.

Dampen the rims of the dishes with a little water.

6. Cut thin strips of puff pastry and press on to the dampened rims. Brush pastry strips with water, add the pastry lids, press edges together well and trim any excess pastry. Cut leaves from trimmings and arrange on top.

To freeze: wrap pies in clingfilm, then seal and label. Freeze for up to 1 month.

To defrost: thaw for 6 hours at room temperature.

To reheat: brush lightly with beaten egg and cook at 200°C, 400°F, Gas 6, for 25 minutes or until the pastry is well risen and an even golden brown.

Serve with steamed carrots, courgettes and sugar peas.

Above: Chicken & Bacon Pie served with steamed carrots, courgettes and sugar peas

P·R·A·C·T·I·C·A·L·I·T·I·E·S

- When making the chicken recipes, batch-cook using the basic recipe, then pack into individual freezerproof dishes or freezer bags. This way you can defrost as many portions as you need, whether it's lunch for one, dinner for two or for entertaining when friends come round.
- Buy ready-portioned chicken pieces or boneless chicken portions as an alternative, if you prefer.
- Remove the skin from the chicken before cooking to reduce the fat content of dish. Alternatively, you could remove the skin and skim the sauce just before serving.

BASIC MINCE RECIPE

1.8 kg (4 lb) lean minced beef
3 large onions, chopped
793 g (1¾ lb) can tomatoes
450 ml (¾ pint) beef stock
1 tbsp granulated sugar
1 tbsp tomato purée
salt and freshly ground black
*   pepper*

PREPARATION: 5 minutes
COOKING: 1 hour 10 minutes

1. Dry-fry mince and onion in a large saucepan for about 10 minutes, stirring occasionally, until mince is evenly browned.
2. Add remaining ingredients and stir well. Bring to boil, then cover and simmer for 1 hour, stirring occasionally.
3. Divide mince mixture into three equal portions for use in the following recipes.

GREEK-STYLE MINCE

SERVES: 4

2 courgettes, diced
⅓ Basic Mince Recipe,
*   prepared as above*
½ tsp grated nutmeg
1 tsp ground cinnamon
To serve:
mixed salad
pitta bread

PREPARATION: 10 minutes
REHEATING: 10 minutes

1. Cook the diced courgettes in lightly salted boiling water

for 1 minute.
2. Drain and stir into the mince mixture, then add the spices. Allow to cool.
To freeze: place individual portions into freezer bags, then seal and label. Freeze for up to 3 months.
To defrost: thaw for 4 hours or use a microwave.
To reheat: bring to boil in a saucepan, cover and cook for 10 minutes, stirring occasionally until piping hot; or use a microwave.

Serve with a mixed salad and pitta bread.

SPICED COTTAGE PIES

SERVES: 4

2 carrots, peeled and chopped
⅓ Basic Mince Recipe,
*   prepared as above*
1 tbsp paprika
775 g (1¾ lb) potatoes, peeled
*   and cut into chunks*
4 tbsp soured cream
25 g (1 oz) butter
2 tsp caraway seeds
salt and freshly ground black
*   pepper*
To serve:
cabbage

PREPARATION: 20 minutes
COOKING: 20 minutes
REHEATING: 40 minutes

1. Cook carrots in lightly salted boiling water for 5 minutes.
2. Drain. Stir into the mince
mixture with the paprika.
Divide between four individual oven/freezerproof dishes.
3. Cook potato chunks in
lightly salted boiling water for
15 minutes or until soft.
4. Drain and mash with the
soured cream and butter. Stir
in the caraway seeds and add
black pepper to taste.

5. Spoon mashed potatoes over
mince and fluff up potato with
a fork. Allow to cool, then dot
with a little butter.
To freeze: wrap dishes in
clingfilm, then seal and label
them. Freeze for up to
3 months.
To defrost: thaw cottage pies
for 5 hours at room
temperature or use a
microwave.
To reheat: cook at 180°C,
350°F, Gas 4, for 40 minutes;
or microwave, and then brown
under the grill.

Serve with cabbage.

*Above: Greek-style Mince served
with a mixed salad and pitta
bread; Spiced Cottage Pies
served with cabbage*

P·R·A·C·T·I·C·A·L·I·T·I·E·S

- Use extra lean minced steak
  or beef which contains less fat
  than ordinary mince.
- You could buy rump steak
  and mince it yourself at home
  if you prefer.
- If you don't have a big
  enough saucepan for cooking
  the basic mince recipe, use
  two pans and transfer the
  mixture to one pan once it
  has reduced down.

F·A·M·I·L·Y M·E·A·L·S

PASTA SAUCE

SERVES: 4

1 clove garlic, crushed
1 red pepper, chopped
⅓ Basic Mince Recipe,
*   prepared as on page 66*
100 g (4 oz) mushrooms,
*   sliced*
2 tsp dried marjoram
To serve:
pasta bows tossed in butter
*   and pesto*

PREPARATION: 10 minutes
REHEATING: 10 minutes

1. Stir garlic and red pepper
into the mince mixture with
the mushrooms and marjoram.
2. Allow to cool thoroughly.
To freeze: put portions into
freezer bags, seal and label.
Freeze for up to 3 months.
To defrost: thaw for 4 hours
or use a microwave.
To reheat: bring to boil in a
saucepan, then cover and cook

Above: Pasta Sauce served with
pasta bows tossed in butter and
pesto

for 10 minutes, stirring
occasionally, or use a
microwave.
   Toss pasta bows in butter
and pesto; serve with sauce.

BEAN & PORK POT ROAST

SERVES: 4-6

2 tbsp olive oil

1 onion, sliced

4 carrots, peeled and sliced

4 sticks celery, sliced

2 cloves garlic, crushed

432 g (15¼ oz) can chickpeas, drained

432 g (15¼ oz) can black-eye beans, drained

397 g (14 oz) can chopped tomatoes

sprig fresh thyme or ¼ tsp dried

salt and freshly ground black pepper

1.5kg (3¼ lb) piece thick end of belly pork

4 baking potatoes, scrubbed

fresh thyme to garnish

40 g (1½ oz) butter

PREPARATION: 30 minutes

COOKING: 1½ hours

1. Preheat the oven to 200°C, 400°F, Gas 6. Heat the oil in a flameproof casserole dish or frying pan. Add the sliced onion, carrots, celery and garlic and fry for 5 minutes until softened.

2. Add drained chickpeas and beans, tomatoes, thyme and seasoning. Bring to the boil, while stirring.

3. Score skin of pork, using a sharp knife, if not already done. Rub in a little salt. Place joint on top of bean mixture if using a flameproof casserole dish, or transfer the bean mixture to a roasting tin and then place the piece of pork on top.

4. Cook, uncovered, in the centre of the oven for 1½ hours until the pork skin is crisp and the juices run clear when the meat is pierced with a skewer.

5. Prick the potatoes, place on the same shelf as the pork and cook for 1½ hours.

6. Transfer the pork to a serving dish and spoon the beans around. Garnish with fresh thyme. Carve the pork.

Serve with baked potatoes, split and buttered.

Below: Bean & Pork Pot Roast

F·A·M·I·L·Y M·E·A·L·S

BASIC CHEESE SAUCE

100 g (4 oz) margarine
100 g (4 oz) plain flour
1 litre (2 pints) skimmed milk
salt and freshly ground black pepper
150 g (6 oz) Cheddar cheese, grated

PREPARATION AND COOKING: 10 minutes

1. Melt margarine and stir in flour. Cook for 1 minute.
2. Gradually whisk in milk and bring to boil, whisking continuously until thickened and smooth. Season well, then stir in grated cheese. Heat until cheese has melted.
3. Cover surface with crumpled and wetted greaseproof paper so that skin doesn't form. Use in the following recipes.

CHEESY BAKED HADDOCK

SERVES: 4

550 g (1¼ lb) smoked haddock
198 g (7 oz) can sweetcorn, drained
450 ml (¾ pint) basic Cheese Sauce, prepared as above
2 tbsp fresh parsley or chives
4 slices of bread, buttered
50 g (2 oz) Cheddar cheese, grated
To serve:
green beans

PREPARATION: 20 minutes
COOKING: 10 minutes
REHEATING: 25 minutes

1. Steam haddock for 10 minutes until fish flakes easily.
2. Stir the sweetcorn into the cheese sauce with the parsley or chives.
3. Skin and break fish into chunky pieces, discarding any bones. Stir into the sauce and spoon into four individual oven/freezerproof dishes.
4. Cut the buttered bread into triangles or fish shapes and place over the fish mixture. Sprinkle with cheese and allow to cool thoroughly.
To freeze: wrap in clingfilm, then seal and label. Freeze for up to 3 months.
To defrost: thaw for 2 hours or use a microwave.
To reheat: cook at 200°C, 400°F, Gas 6, for 25 minutes or until bread is browned; or microwave and brown under a preheated grill.
    Serve with green beans.

P·R·A·C·T·I·C·A·L·I·T·I·E·S

• Smoked haddock is sometimes quite salty, so leave it to soak in milk for an hour before making the Cheesy Baked Haddock. Or you could make the recipe with unsmoked fish such as haddock, cod or coley.
• To save time, you could buy ready-grated Cheddar cheese, available from supermarkets.
• If liked, make Cheesy Baked Haddock with cooked frozen peas instead of sweetcorn.

NUTTY PASTA BAKE

SERVES: 4

325 g (12 oz) pasta whirls
225 g (8 oz) streaky bacon, derinded and chopped
1 tsp oil
½ bunch spring onions, chopped
100 g (4 oz) Cheddar cheese, grated
1 tsp mustard
625 ml (1¼ pints) basic Cheese Sauce, prepared as left
25 g (1 oz) almonds
To serve:
sweetcorn

PREPARATION: 20 minutes
COOKING: 10 minutes
REHEATING: 25 minutes

1. Cook the pasta whirls in plenty of lightly salted boiling water for 8-10 minutes, until the pasta is just tender. Drain thoroughly.

2. Fry the streaky bacon in the oil until golden. Add the chopped spring onions and cook for 2 minutes.

3. Stir 50 g (2 oz) of the grated cheese and the mustard into the cheese sauce.

4. Drain the bacon and onions and add to sauce with the

pasta. Mix together and spoon into four individual oven/freezerproof dishes. Sprinkle with the almonds and remaining grated cheese. Allow to cool.

To freeze: open-freeze until solid. Wrap in clingfilm, seal, label. Freeze for up to 1 month.

To defrost: thaw for 2 hours or use a microwave.

To reheat: cook at 200° C, 400° F, Gas 6, for 25 minutes until golden.

Serve with sweetcorn.

VEGGIE MOUSSAKA

SERVES: 4

1 onion, sliced
2 tbsp olive oil
1 small aubergine, diced
2 courgettes, diced
397 g (14 oz) can tomatoes
½ tsp dried oregano
½ tsp sugar
salt and freshly ground black
    pepper
250 g (9 oz) broccoli, broken
    into florets
675 g (1½ lb) potatoes,
    scrubbed and sliced
3 tbsp milk
300 ml (½ pint) basic Cheese
    Sauce, prepared as opposite
2 tbsp Parmesan cheese
To serve:
green salad

Left to right: Cheesy Baked Haddock, Nutty Pasta Bake and Veggie Moussaka

PREPARATION: 20 minutes
COOKING: 20 minutes
REHEATING: 25 minutes

1. Fry the sliced onion in the oil until softened. Add the diced aubergine and courgettes to the onion and fry gently for 5 minutes.

2. Add the tomatoes, oregano, sugar and seasoning. Cover and simmer for 10 minutes.

3. Add the broccoli to the vegetable mixture and cook, uncovered, for 5 minutes until the broccoli is almost tender.

4. Cook the potato slices in lightly salted boiling water for 5 minutes.

5. Divide the vegetable mixture between four individual oven/freezerproof dishes. Drain the potatoes well and arrange over the top of each dish.

6. Add the milk to the cheese sauce and pour over dishes. Sprinkle with Parmesan cheese.

To freeze: open-freeze until solid. Wrap in clingfilm, seal, label. Freeze for up to 3 months.

To defrost: thaw moussaka for 3 hours at room temperature, or use a microwave.

To reheat: cook at 200° C, 400° F, Gas 6, for 25 minutes until the top is browned; or use a microwave and brown under a preheated grill.

Serve with a green salad.

F·A·M·I·L·Y M·E·A·L·S

FAMILY LASAGNE

SERVES: 4-6

Filling:

450 g (1 lb) lean minced beef

1 onion, chopped

2 cloves garlic, crushed

150 g (6 oz) green lentils, washed

397 g (14 oz) can chopped tomatoes

2 tbsp tomato purée

300 ml (½ pint) beef stock

1 tsp dried marjoram

salt and freshly ground black pepper

1 small red pepper, deseeded and finely chopped

1 small green pepper, deseeded and finely chopped

1 small yellow pepper, deseeded and finely chopped

Sauce:

50 g (2 oz) butter

50 g (2 oz) plain flour

600 ml (1 pint) milk

pinch grated nutmeg

salt and freshly ground black pepper

To finish:

8 sheets no-cook lasagne

50 g (2 oz) Cheddar cheese, grated

2 tbsp Parmesan cheese

2 tbsp fresh breadcrumbs

To serve:

mixed salad

crusty bread

PREPARATION: 45 minutes
COOKING: 1½-2 hours

1. Dry-fry the mince and the chopped onion in a large saucepan, stirring well until evenly browned.

2. Add the garlic, lentils, tomatoes, tomato purée, stock, marjoram and seasoning. Bring to the boil, stirring.

3. Simmer the mince uncovered for 25 minutes, stirring occasionally.

4. To make the sauce, heat the butter in a separate pan. Stir in the flour and cook for 1 minute. Gradually stir in the milk and bring to the boil, stirring continuously until the sauce is thickened and smooth. Stir in the grated nutmeg and seasoning.

5. Preheat the oven to 160°C, 325°F, Gas 3. Stir the peppers into the mince mixture.

6. Spoon half the mince mixture into the base of a shallow ovenproof dish. Spoon one-third of the sauce over mixture, then cover with half the lasagne sheets, breaking the sheets up if necessary, to fit the dish.

7. Repeat the layers of mince, sauce and lasagne, and top with the remaining sauce. Sprinkle with the Cheddar and Parmesan cheese and breadcrumbs.

8. Cover the dish loosely with oiled foil and cook in the centre of the oven for 1½-2 hours.

9. Brown the top of the lasagne under a hot grill and serve with a mixed salad and warm crusty bread.

LEEK & HAM BAKE

SERVES: 4

75 g (3 oz) butter

50 g (2 oz) plain flour

600 ml (1 pint) milk

225 g (8 oz) Cheddar cheese, grated

1 tsp coarse-grain mustard

salt and freshly ground black pepper

198 g (7 oz) can sweetcorn, drained

275 g (10 oz) thick piece ham, diced

450 g (1 lb) leeks, cut into 2.5 cm (1 inch) lengths

550 g (1¼ lb) potatoes, scrubbed and sliced

PREPARATION: 35 minutes
COOKING: 1½-2 hours

1. Preheat the oven to 160°C,
325°F, Gas 3. Melt 50 g
(2 oz) butter in a saucepan.
Stir in the flour and cook for
1 minute.
2. Gradually add the milk and
bring to the boil, stirring until
the sauce is thickened and
smooth.
3. Stir in 150 g (6 oz) grated
cheese, mustard and
seasoning, and heat until the
cheese has melted.
4. Stir in the sweetcorn, ham
and leeks. Pour into a shallow
ovenproof dish.
5. Cook potatoes in boiling
water for 2 minutes. Drain,

Above: Leek & Ham Bake

rinsé with cold water and
drain again.
6. Overlap the potatoes in
layers on top of mixture.
7. Melt the remaining butter
and brush over a large piece of
foil and over the potatoes.
Sprinkle the potatoes with
remaining cheese and loosely
cover with foil.
8. Cook in the centre of the
oven for 1½-2 hours. Remove
the foil and brown the top
under a hot grill. Serve hot.

*Left: Family Lasagne served with
a mixed salad and warm crusty
bread*

SPICED PORK SALAD

SERVES: *2*

2 Little Gem lettuces
50 g (2 oz) young spinach,
  leaves only
½ bunch watercress
1 nectarine, halved and
  stoned
225 g (8 oz) pork fillet,
  thinly sliced
salt and freshly ground black
  pepper
1 tbsp oil
4 tbsp natural yogurt
1 tbsp milk
½-1 tsp mild curry paste

PREPARATION: 20 minutes
COOKING: 8 minutes

1. Separate the Little Gem
lettuces into leaves, then, with
the spinach, tear into bite-
sized pieces. Trim the
watercress. Wash all three lots
of leaves thoroughly, then
drain and dry. Put them
together in a large bowl.
2. Chop the nectarine into
cubes. Mix with the leaves.
3. Season the pork and fry in
oil for 8 minutes, turning once
until evenly browned and
cooked right through.
  Transfer the pork to the
leaves using a slotted spoon.
Toss together and spoon on to
two plates.
4. Mix the natural yogurt,
milk and curry paste together.
Drizzle over the mixed leaves.
Serve immediately.

SALAD NIÇOISE

SERVES: *2*

2 eggs
50 g (2 oz) green beans,
  trimmed and halved
3 tbsp oil
1 tbsp lemon juice
freshly ground black pepper
50 g (1¼ oz) can anchovies,
  drained
185 g (6½ oz) can tuna in
  brine, drained
6 stoned black olives
1 tbsp fresh chopped
  parsley
⅓ iceberg lettuce, shredded
2 tomatoes, cut into wedges
To serve:
crusty bread

PREPARATION: 15 minutes
COOKING: 10 minutes

1. Put eggs in pan of cold
water, bring to boil, then
simmer for 10 minutes. Steam
beans over an egg pan for
4 minutes. Rinse in cold
water, drain and set aside.
2. Mix together the oil, lemon
juice and plenty of black
pepper to make dressing.
3. Add the anchovies and tuna
to bowl of dressing, breaking
tuna into pieces. Add beans,
olives and parsley and toss
together lightly with the
lettuce and tomatoes.
4. Drain eggs, crack shells and
run under cold water until
they are cool enough to
handle. Peel off shells and cut
eggs into quarters. Add to
salad and toss together lightly.
  Spoon on to two plates and
serve with crusty bread.

THREE-CHEESE SALAD

SERVES: *2*

200 g (7 oz) packet mixed
  salad leaves
1 avocado
2 tsp lemon juice
75 g (3 oz) Jarlsberg cheese
75 g (3 oz) smoked Edam
  cheese
75 g (3 oz) white Cheshire
  cheese
2 tbsp walnut pieces
6 tbsp oil
4 tsp white wine vinegar
1 tsp Dijon mustard
salt and freshly ground black
  pepper

PREPARATION: 20 minutes

1. Tear salad leaves into small
pieces. Halve avocado, remove
stone and peel. Chop up into
cubes, toss in lemon juice and
then add to leaves. Spoon on
to two plates.
2. Thinly slice the cheeses and
arrange over leaves.
3. Grill walnut pieces lightly.
Mix oil, vinegar, mustard and
seasoning together. Add hot
walnuts, mix together and
spoon over salad.
  Serve with crusty bread.

Right (clockwise): Spiced Pork
Salad; Salad Niçoise; Three-
Cheese Salad

·CHAPTER 6·

P·U·D·D·I·N·G·S
& D·E·S·S·E·R·T·S

*'What's for pudding, Mum?' is a familiar cry from
the kids who always want to know the answer before
you've even dished out the first course. This
mouthwatering selection of puddings and desserts
should keep them sweet – and you'll find these recipes
will go down well with adults, too!*

CARAMEL & BANANA CUSTARDS

SERVES: 5-6

125 g (5 oz) caster sugar
2 tbsp water
1 large banana
450 ml (¾ pint) milk
4 eggs
To serve:
cream, optional

PREPARATION: 15 minutes
(plus chilling time)
COOKING: 55 minutes

1. Preheat the oven to 180°C,
350°F, Gas 4. Place 100 g
(4 oz) sugar in a small heavy-
based saucepan. Add the water
and heat gently until sugar
dissolves. Bring to the boil
and boil rapidly for 8 minutes
or until caramel is dark golden
in colour.
2. Pour caramel into five or
six individual ramekin dishes.
3. Break banana into pieces
and place in a food processor
or blender with the milk, eggs
and remaining sugar. Blend
until mixture is smooth.
4. Pour banana mixture over
caramel. Stand dishes in a
roasting tin, then fill tin with
boiling water to come halfway
up sides of ramekins. Bake for
45 minutes or until surfaces
feel lightly set to the touch.
5. Leave to cool then chill for

*Left: Caramel & Banana
Custards*

several hours. Loosen edges with knife then turn out on to serving plates.

Serve with cream, if liked.

BANANA PANCAKES WITH BUTTERSCOTCH SAUCE

SERVES: 6

Sauce:

150 g (6 oz) demerara sugar
3 tbsp golden syrup
150 ml (¼ pint) water
50 g (2 oz) butter
¼ tsp vanilla essence
1 tsp lemon juice
2 tbsp milk

Pancakes:

100 g (4 oz) plain flour
pinch of salt
1 egg
1 egg yolk
2 tbsp oil, plus extra for frying
300 ml (½ pint) milk
4 large bananas, thinly sliced

To serve:

ice-cream

PREPARATION: 15 minutes
COOKING: 40 minutes

1. To make the sauce, heat the sugar, syrup and water gently in a saucepan until the sugar has completely dissolved.

2. Bring to the boil and boil rapidly for 5 minutes, without stirring, until toffee-coloured and syrupy. Remove the pan from the heat.

3. Add butter. When melted,

add the vanilla essence, lemon juice and milk; stir well. Leave to cool slightly.

4. To make pancakes, sift flour and salt into a bowl. Add the egg, egg yolk, 2 tbsp oil and a little of the milk. Whisk until smooth. Gradually whisk in the remaining milk.

5. Heat a little oil in the base of an 18 cm (7 inch) non-stick frying pan. Pour off almost all the oil and add about 2 tbsp of the pancake batter, tilting pan until base is thinly covered.

6. Cook for 2 minutes or until the underside is golden. Loosen edge with a palette knife and turn over. Cook for 1-2 minutes.

Above: Banana Pancakes with Butterscotch Sauce served with ice-cream

7. Slide out of pan on to some greaseproof paper. Cover with foil to keep warm.

8. Repeat until all of the pancake batter is used up, interleaving the pancakes with greaseproof paper.

9. Fold the pancakes into triangles; arrange on serving plates and divide banana slices between them.

10. Reheat sauce, if preferred, but test temperature before serving to children. Spoon a little over pancakes and serve with ice-cream.

P·U·D·D·I·N·G·S & D·E·S·S·E·R·T·S

FLUFFY TOPPED RICE PUDDING

SERVES: 6

50 g (2 oz) pudding rice
600 ml (1 pint) milk
25 g (1 oz) butter
25 g (1 oz) caster sugar
50 g (2 oz) mixed dried fruit
2 egg whites

PREPARATION: 10 minutes
COOKING: 1 hour 20 minutes

1. Preheat the oven to 200°C, 400°F, Gas 6. Place rice, milk, butter and sugar in a saucepan. Bring to the boil and simmer gently, covered, until the rice is tender, about 1 hour.
2. Stir in mixed dried fruit. Beat egg whites until holding their shape.
3. Carefully fold the egg whites into the rice mixture

Above: Fluffy Topped Rice Pudding

using a metal tablespoon.
4. Turn into lightly greased, shallow baking dish. Cook for about 20 minutes until risen and golden.

OLD-FASHIONED TRIFLE

SERVES: 6

4 trifle sponges
3 tbsp raspberry or
  strawberry jam
225 g (8 oz) frozen
  raspberries, thawed
150 ml (¼ pint) fresh orange
  or apple juice
600 ml (1 pint) milk
3 tbsp custard powder
2 tbsp caster sugar
150 ml (¼ pint) double
  cream
raspberries to decorate

PREPARATION: 20 minutes
(plus chilling time)

1. Halve each sponge and sandwich with jam. Cut into cubes; place in six individual dishes or one large dish.
2. Scatter with raspberries, then drizzle with fruit juice.
3. Blend a little of the milk with custard powder and sugar. Bring remaining milk to boil then pour over custard mixture, stirring. Return to pan and cook, stirring continuously, until thickened.
4. Leave to cool slightly then spoon over trifles. Leave until custard has set.
5. Whip cream until just holding its shape. Place in piping bag fitted with large star nozzle and use to decorate trifles. Top with raspberries.

Old-fashioned Trifle

BREAD & BUTTER PUDDING

SERVES: 6

25 g (1 oz) butter
8 slices white bread
50 g (2 oz) sultanas
3 eggs
450 ml (¾ pint) milk
1 tsp vanilla essence
50 g (2 oz) caster sugar
icing sugar, for dusting

PREPARATION: 15 minutes
(plus 1 hour standing time)
COOKING: 1 hour

Above: Bread & Butter Pudding

1. Lightly grease large baking dish. Butter the bread and cut into quarters. Layer up in dish, sprinkling layers with the sultanas.
2. Beat eggs with the milk, vanilla essence and sugar. Spoon over the bread. Leave to stand for 1 hour; bake at 180°C, 350°F, Gas 4, for 1 hour until golden.
3. Serve, dusted with a little icing sugar.

GOOSEBERRY FOOL

SERVES: 6

2 x 300 g (11 oz) jars
    gooseberries in syrup,
    drained
4 tbsp icing sugar
425 g (15 oz) can low-fat
    custard
6 tbsp strained Greek
    yogurt
To serve:
wafer biscuits

PREPARATION: 20 minutes

1. Reserve a few gooseberries
for decoration and process or
liquidize remainder. Press
through a sieve into a bowl.
2. Mix the gooseberry purée,
icing sugar and custard
together. Add yogurt and mix
lightly to give the fool a
marbled appearance.
3. Spoon into glass serving
dishes. Decorate with reserved
gooseberries and serve with
wafer biscuits.

*Below: Gooseberry Fool served
with wafer biscuits*

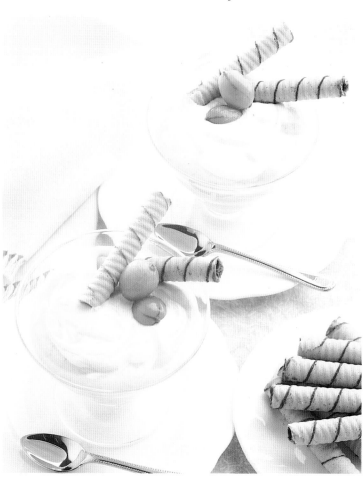

APRICOT & ALMOND TOPSY-TURVY

SERVES: 6

3 tbsp flaked almonds
125 g (5 oz) light muscovado
    sugar
2 x 411 g (14½ oz) cans
    apricot halves in natural
    juice, drained
75 g (3 oz) caster sugar
150 g (6 oz) self-raising flour
150 g (6 oz) soft margarine
3 eggs, beaten
1½ tsp baking powder
¼ tsp almond essence
50 g (2 oz) ground almonds
2 tbsp milk
To serve:
whipped cream or custard

PREPARATION: 20 minutes
COOKING: 40 minutes

1. Preheat the oven to 180°C,
350°F, Gas 4. Grease and line
the base of an 18 x 28 x 4 cm
(7 x 11 x 1½ inch) tin using a
sheet of greased greaseproof
paper cut to size.
2. Sprinkle flaked almonds
over the base of tin and follow
with 50 g (2 oz) sprinkling of
muscovado sugar.
3. Arrange all the apricots in
the baking tin, cut side
uppermost.
4. Put all the remaining
ingredients except the ground
almonds and milk in a bowl or
food processor and mix
together until smooth.
5. Add the ground almonds

and milk, and mix well.

6. Drop spoonfuls of the mixture over the apricots and then level the surface carefully with a knife.

7. Cook for about 40 minutes, or until sponge is golden brown and springs back when pressed with the fingertips.

8. Leave to cool in the tin for 10-15 minutes. Loosen edges with a knife and turn out on to a large serving plate.

Cut sponge into squares and serve with whipped cream or custard.

P·R·A·C·T·I·C·A·L·I·T·I·E·S

• If there are less than six people for pudding, make the Spiced Apple Pie and Pear & Blackberry Crumble (page 83) in two small dishes and freeze one for another day.
• Cut into small bars, the Topsy-Turvy is ideal for kids' lunchboxes.

Above: Apricot & Almond Topsy-Turvy served with cream
Right: Spiced Apple Pie served with vanilla ice-cream

SPICED APPLE PIE

SERVES: 6

1.1 kg (2½ lb) cooking apples, peeled, quartered and cored
2 tbsp lemon juice
1 tsp ground cinnamon
50 g (2 oz) sultanas
3 tbsp clear honey
370 g (13 oz) packet frozen puff pastry, just thawed
1 egg, beaten
caster sugar, for sprinkling
To serve:
ice-cream

PREPARATION: 40 minutes
COOKING: 30 minutes

1. Preheat the oven to 200°C, 400°F, Gas 6. Cut the apples into thick slices and put into a 1.2 litre (2 pint) pie dish. Add the lemon juice, cinnamon, sultanas and honey and toss together well.

2. Roll out pastry thinly on a lightly floured surface until about 7.5 cm (3 inches) larger than the top of the pie dish.

3. Brush edge of pie dish with a little beaten egg. Cut strips of pastry and press them on to edge of dish.

4. Brush pastry strips with egg. Lift pastry over a rolling pin and position over fruit. Press edges together well to seal and trim. Knock up pastry edge with a small knife and flute.

5. Brush pie with egg and decorate with animal shapes cut from pastry trimmings. Brush with rest of egg then sprinkle pie with caster sugar.

6. Cook for about 30 minutes until well risen and golden. Check after 15 minutes and cover pastry animals with foil if overbrowning.

Serve warm with ice-cream.

ORANGE & KIWI CHEESECAKE

SERVES: 6

100 g (4 oz) Nice biscuits
25 g (1 oz) butter
1 tbsp golden syrup
142 g (5 oz) tablet tangerine jelly
200 g (7 oz) tub low-fat soft cheese
2 oranges
300 ml (½ pint) whipping cream
2 kiwi fruit, peeled and thinly sliced

PREPARATION: 20 minutes (plus 3 hours chilling)

1. Place the Nice biscuits into a plastic bag; seal bag and crush biscuits finely with a heavy rolling pin.

2. Heat the butter and syrup in a saucepan or in a bowl in the microwave on Full Power (100%) for 1 minute until butter has melted.

3. Stir in biscuits and mix well. Spoon into the base of a lightly oiled 20 cm (8 inch) springform tin and press down firmly with the end of a rolling pin. Chill until base is required.

4. Cut jelly into small pieces and dissolve in boiling water. Top up to 300 ml (½ pint) with cold water. Leave to cool.

5. Put soft cheese into a bowl. Add the grated rind of one orange. Peel and cut both oranges into segments. Reserve all the segments for final decoration and squeeze juice from the remaining white pith and core. Beat cheese and orange together.

6. Gradually beat the cold, unset jelly into soft cheese mixture.

7. Whip cream in a separate bowl until softly peaking. Fold into cheese mixture and then pour into tin. Smooth surface and chill for 3 hours or until firmly set.

8. Remove cheesecake from tin and place on a serving plate. Arrange kiwi fruit slices and orange segments alternately on top of the cheesecake. Chill until required.

Below: Orange & Kiwi Cheesecake

4. Spoon crumble mixture over to completely cover the fruit. Sprinkle top with remaining sesame seeds.

5. Cook for 40 minutes, until golden.

Serve hot with custard or pouring cream.

MINI FRUIT BASKETS

SERVES: 2

2 kiwi fruit
1 orange, peeled
50 g (2 oz) redcurrants

PREPARATION: 10 minutes

1. Cut 2 wedges from each kiwi fruit to make a basket, leaving a small central band for handle. Scoop out flesh and finely chop.

2. Cut out orange flesh from between membranes, roughly dice. Mix in a bowl with the kiwi fruit and redcurrants.

3. Pack fruit into kiwi fruit baskets and serve.

Mini Fruit Baskets

PEAR & BLACKBERRY CRUMBLE

SERVES: 6

100 g (4 oz) plain flour
50 g (2 oz) porridge oats
100 g (4 oz) demerara sugar
75 g (3 oz) block margarine
3 tbsp sesame seeds
900 g (2 lb) pears, peeled,
  quartered and cored
225 g (8 oz) frozen
  blackberries, just thawed
To serve:
custard or pouring cream

PREPARATION: 25 minutes
COOKING: 40 minutes

1. Preheat the oven to 180°C, 350°F, Gas 4. Put flour, porridge oats and half the demerara sugar into a large bowl or food processor. Add the margarine cut into pieces and then rub in or process

Above: Pear & Blackberry Crumble served with custard

gently until the mixture resembles fine crumbs.

2. Stir in 2 tbsp sesame seeds and set aside.

3. Thickly slice the pears and put into a 1.2 litre (2 pint) deep ovenproof dish with blackberries and remaining demerara sugar.

HONEY & ORANGE SPONGE

SERVES: 6

2 tsp golden syrup
2 tbsp clear honey
150 g (6 oz) self-raising flour
100 g (4 oz) caster sugar
100 g (4 oz) soft margarine
2 eggs
finely grated rind of 1 orange
To serve:
custard or pouring cream

PREPARATION: 20 minutes
COOKING: 2 hours

1. Lightly grease 1.2 litre (2 pint) fluted mould or pudding basin. Pour in golden syrup and honey.
2. Sift flour into a bowl. Add remaining ingredients and beat well until smooth. Spoon into basin and level surface.
3. Cover top of mould or basin with greased greaseproof paper and foil, securing with string under rim.
4. Place on upturned saucer in large saucepan containing 5 cm (2 inches) boiling water. Cover with tight-fitting lid and steam gently for 2 hours, adding more water when necessary.
5. Remove foil and greaseproof paper and turn pudding out on to plate. Serve with custard or pouring cream.

Right: Honey & Orange Sponge
Far right top: Hot Fruit Salad
Far right bottom: No-Bake Chocolate Cake

HOT FRUIT SALAD

SERVES: 6

1 small pineapple
2 satsumas or tangerines, peeled
2 red-skinned dessert apples, cored and sliced
1 green-skinned dessert apple, cored and sliced
2 tbsp long-thread or desiccated coconut
50 g (2 oz) butter
50 g (2 oz) demerara sugar
2 tbsp sherry or apple juice
To serve:
natural yogurt

PREPARATION: 15 minutes
COOKING: 5 minutes

1. Cut pineapple into quarters. Cut away skin and core, then cut fruit into bite-sized pieces.
2. Break satsumas or tangerines into segments and then cut each one in half. Set aside with apple slices.
3. Put coconut into a saucepan and heat gently, stirring frequently until lightly browned. Take out of pan and reserve.
4. Heat the butter in a saucepan until just melted. Add all the fruit, sugar, sherry or apple juice and cook for 5 minutes, stirring until hot but not browned.
5. Spoon into serving dishes and sprinkle with coconut. Serve with natural yogurt.

NO-BAKE CHOCOLATE CAKE

SERVES: 16

a little oil
200 g (7 oz) Rich Tea
  biscuits
200 g (7 oz) plain chocolate-
  flavoured cake covering
100 g (4 oz) plain chocolate
50 g (2 oz) butter
3 tbsp golden syrup
100 g (4 oz) glacé cherries,
  roughly chopped
100 g (4 oz) sugar-rolled
  chopped dates

PREPARATION: 5 minutes
(plus 4 hours chilling)
COOKING: 2 minutes

1. Lightly brush base and sides of an 18 cm (7 inch) deep, loose-bottomed fluted flan tin with a small amount of oil.
2. Put biscuits in a plastic bag and crush with a rolling pin.
3. Break the chocolate-flavoured cake covering and the plain chocolate into pieces, put into a large microwave-proof bowl with the butter and the golden syrup.
4. Microwave on High (100%) for 2 minutes until melted. Stir well. Alternatively, put cake covering and plain chocolate pieces into a saucepan with the butter and golden syrup and heat gently, stirring until melted. Remove from heat.
5. Add biscuits, cherries and dates and stir well until evenly coated in chocolate.
6. Spoon into flan tin. Level surface with back of a spoon. Chill for 4 hours until set.
7. Remove flan tin, cut cake into thin wedges and serve.

P·R·A·C·T·I·C·A·L·I·T·I·E·S

- Plain digestive or oat biscuits can replace Rich Tea biscuits.
- Natural yogurt is a healthier option than cream for serving with puddings, and custard is a good way of encouraging children to take more milk.

P·U·D·D·I·N·G·S & D·E·S·S·E·R·T·S

downwards into basin. Dip strips of bread into the juice and place overlapping around sides of basin until sides are completely covered. Press edges together to seal.

5. Spoon in fruits then dip remaining strips of bread in juice and use to cover top of pudding. Pour over half the remaining juice.

6. Stand basin on a plate and cover top of pudding with a second plate. Weight the top plate with a bag of flour or sugar and transfer to the fridge to chill overnight.

7. Just before serving, remove plates and loosen edge of pudding. Turn out on to a serving plate and decorate with extra fruit if using. Serve immediately with cream.

SUMMER PUDDING

SERVES: 6

900 g (2 lb) mixed
   strawberries, raspberries
   and redcurrants
75 g (3 oz) caster sugar
150 ml (¼ pint) water
12 slices white bread
To serve:
extra strawberries,
   raspberries, redcurrants,
   optional
cream

PREPARATION: 30 minutes
(plus chilling overnight)
COOKING: 5 minutes

Above: Summer Pudding served with cream

1. Hull strawberries and raspberries, string redcurrants. Put into a saucepan with the sugar and water. Simmer gently for 4-5 minutes until fruits are just soft.

2. Drain fruits in a colander and save juice.

3. Trim the crusts from the bread. Cut a circle to fit the base of a 1.1 litre (2 pint) basin and cut the remaining bread into thick strips.

4. Dip a circle of bread into juice then place dipped side

STRAWBERRY CREAM PIE

SERVES: 6-8

Base:
150 g (6 oz) malted milk
   biscuits
50 g (2 oz) butter
1 tbsp golden syrup
Filling:
packet strawberry jelly
150 ml (¼ pint) boiling water
425 g (15 oz) can low-fat
   custard
325 g (12 oz) strawberries
150 ml (¼ pint) double cream

PREPARATION: 50 minutes
CHILLING: 4-5 hours

1. To make the base, place the malted milk biscuits in a plastic bag and crush with a rolling pin until they resemble fine breadcrumbs.

2. Heat butter and golden syrup in a saucepan until butter has melted. Stir in biscuit crumbs and mix well.

3. Butter an 18 cm (7 inch) deep, loose-bottomed flan tin. Spoon in crumbs and press firmly and evenly into the base and sides of tin. Chill.

4. To make filling, cut strawberry jelly into small pieces and dissolve in boiling water. Make up to 300 ml (½ pint) with cold water. Cool.

5. Stir custard into jelly and pour mixture on to biscuit base. Chill for 4-5 hours until firmly set.

6. Reserving 4 strawberries for decoration, hull and slice the remainder. Arrange slices over the top of the filling.

7. Whip the double cream until softly peaking, then spoon two-thirds over the strawberries and spread evenly with a knife.

8. Loosen edges of pie with a knife, carefully stand flan tin on a can and remove ring. Place on a serving plate, loosen metal base and carefully slide away using a knife to help.

9. Spoon remaining cream around edge of pie using a teaspoon and decorate with reserved halved strawberries.

TANGY ICE-CREAM WITH FUDGE SAUCE

SERVES: 8

3 oranges
1 tbsp clear honey
50 g (2 oz) caster sugar
1 tbsp cornflour
150 ml (¼ pint) water
300 ml (½ pint) double cream
Fudge sauce:
50 g (2 oz) plain chocolate
4 tsp golden syrup
50 g (2 oz) butter or
  margarine
2 tsp water
To decorate:
orange slices
Smarties

PREPARATION: 25 minutes (plus freezing overnight)
COOKING: 5 minutes

1. Grate rind from oranges and reserve. Peel oranges and roughly slice flesh.

2. Place the orange flesh in a food processor or blender with the grated orange zest, honey, caster sugar and cornflour and blend until smooth.

3. Transfer to a saucepan and stir in the water. Bring to the boil, stirring until thickened. Cook for 1 minute. Leave to cool completely.

4. Whip cream until peaking. Fold in orange mixture using a metal tablespoon. Turn into a freezer container and freeze overnight until firm.

5. To make fudge sauce, break

Above: Strawberry Cream Pie
Below: Tangy Ice-cream with Fudge Sauce

up chocolate and place in a small pan with the syrup, butter or margarine and water. Heat gently, stirring until chocolate has completely melted and mixture is smooth.

6. Remove ice-cream from freezer. Scoop balls of ice-cream into serving tumblers or bowls, decorating with orange slices and Smarties. Reheat fudge sauce if necessary and spoon it over the ice-cream.

C·H·I·L·D·R·E·N'S

P·A·R·T·I·E·S

No children's party is complete without tea-time treats. Whether you're planning simple snacks or a full-scale spread for your child's party, this selection of mouthwatering ideas should help things go with a swing. Your child will also enjoy helping you to prepare the simpler recipes.

CRISPY SNAILS

MAKES: 30

500 g (1 lb 2 oz) packet puff
   pastry, thawed if frozen
1 egg, beaten
12 thin slices chopped ham
   loaf with peppers
12 slices processed cheese
To decorate:
celery leaves

PREPARATION: 25 minutes
COOKING: 10 minutes

1. Preheat the oven to 220°C,
425°F, Gas 7. On a lightly
floured surface roll out half of

pastry thinly, trim to rectangle 33 x 25 cm (13 x 10 inches).

2. Brush pastry with egg and top with six slices ham and then six slices cheese.

3. Roll up pastry from longest edge, like a Swiss roll. Cut into slices and lie them flat on a lightly greased baking sheet. Repeat the procedure with the remaining ingredients.

4. Brush tops of slices with egg. Cook for about 10 minutes until pastry is well risen and golden.

5. Serve warm on a plate decorated with celery leaves.

POOH STICKS

MAKES: 80

a little oil
325 g (12 oz) plain flour
salt and freshly ground black
  pepper
150 g (6 oz) butter or
  margarine
150 g (6 oz) Cheddar cheese,
  finely grated
2 eggs, beaten

PREPARATION: 20 minutes
COOKING: 10 minutes

1. Preheat the oven to 200°C, 400°F, Gas 6. Lightly brush two baking sheets with oil.
2. Put the flour and a little seasoning into a bowl. Cut the butter or margarine into pieces, then rub into the flour with fingertips until mixture

Left: Crispy Snails

resembles fine crumbs.
3. Stir 100 g (4 oz) of the grated cheese into the flour.
4. Reserving a tablespoonful of the beaten egg, add the remainder to the flour and mix to a smooth dough.
5. Knead on a floured surface, roll out to 5 mm (¼ inch) thick. Cut into 10 cm (4 inch) long sticks; place on baking sheets.
6. Repeat with trimmings.
7. Brush sticks with reserved egg, sprinkle with remaining

Above: Pooh Sticks

cheese. Cook for 10 minutes until golden. Leave to cool.
8. Serve in paper cups.

P·R·A·C·T·I·C·A·L·I·T·I·E·S

- Crispy Snails taste just as good made with slices of plain lean ham.
- Carrot and cucumber sticks or cauliflower florets are ideal healthy finger foods for both children and adults.

TEDDY BEAR SANDWICHES

MAKES: 12

100 g (4 oz) Red Leicester
  cheese, thinly sliced
3 slices ham
12 slices soft-grain white
  bread, spread with
  sunflower margarine
teddy bear cutters
To decorate:
mustard and cress, optional

PREPARATION: 5 minutes

1. Use the fillings to make
three cheese and three ham
sandwiches. Stamp out twelve
bear shapes, two from each
sandwich.
2. Serve decorated with
mustard and cress, if liked.

Above: Teddy Bear Sandwiches
Below: Starry Soup served with
mini moon and star sandwiches

STARRY SOUP

SERVES: 6

900 g (2 lb) tomatoes
2 tbsp olive oil
1 onion, chopped
1 carrot, chopped
2 sticks celery, chopped
1 clove garlic, crushed,
  optional
75 g (3 oz) red lentils
1 tsp paprika
1 tsp sugar
salt and freshly ground black
  pepper
600 ml (1 pint) chicken stock
25 g (1 oz) pasta stars
450 ml (¾ pint) milk
To serve:
mini sandwiches cut into
  moon and star shapes

PREPARATION: 20 minutes
COOKING: 45 minutes

1. Score a cross in the base of each tomato, then put tomatoes into a bowl and cover with boiling water. Leave to soak for 30 seconds or until tomato skins begin to peel away from flesh.

2. Drain tomatoes, put in bowl of cold water. Remove one by one, peel away skin, chop flesh.

3. Heat oil in large saucepan, add onion, carrot and celery. Fry for 5 minutes, stirring occasionally, until softened.

4. Add tomatoes and garlic, if using, and fry for 5 minutes more. Stir in lentils, paprika, sugar and seasoning. Pour on stock, bring to the boil then simmer for 30 minutes.

5. Meanwhile, cook pasta stars in lightly salted boiling water for 10 minutes, then drain.

6. Cool soup slightly then liquidize, process or sieve until smooth.

7. Return soup to saucepan, stir in milk and reheat. Add pasta shapes and ladle into paper cups or bowls. Cool soup slightly before serving to children. Serve with mini moon and star sandwiches.

P·R·A·C·T·I·C·A·L·I·T·I·E·S

- If your child is helping you to prepare food, dress her in an overall or apron and provide a sturdy stool for her to stand on to reach the work surface.
- Always supervise children when cooking and never leave them alone in the kitchen.

STRAWBERRY SHAKES

MAKES: 6

100 g (4 oz) strawberries, hulled and washed
150 g (6 oz) strawberry yogurt
600 ml (1 pint) milk

PREPARATION: 3 minutes

1. Put strawberries and yogurt into a liquidizer or food processor and mix until smooth.

2. Add milk and mix again. Strain if desired.

3. Pour into paper cups and serve with straws.

Below: Strawberry Shakes

POTATO SKINS & AVOCADO DIP

SERVES: 6

1.5 kg (3 lb 5 oz) potatoes, scrubbed
5 tbsp oil
Dip:
2 avocados
½ small onion, quartered
juice of ½ lemon
3 tbsp mayonnaise
few drops chilli sauce
2 tbsp freshly chopped coriander leaves
To garnish:
sprig of fresh coriander

PREPARATION: 20 minutes
COOKING: 1½ hours

1. Preheat the oven to 220°C, 425°F, Gas 7. Prick potatoes, place in a roasting tin and bake for 1 hour or until soft.
2. Leave potatoes to cool slightly then cut them into

Above: Potato Skins & Avocado Dip; Fruit Punch

quarters and scoop out all the soft potato.
3. Put skins into roasting tin and set aside until just before you're ready to eat. (Use the potato as mash or for making fish cakes.)
4. Brush potato skins with oil. Bake for about 30 minutes until crisp.
5. Meanwhile, make the dip. Halve avocados, remove stone and scoop out flesh into a liquidizer or food processor, discarding skins. Add onion quarters to avocado with all the remaining ingredients. Liquidize until just smooth.
6. Spoon dip into a small dish, garnish with coriander and place in the centre of a large plate. Arrange potato skins around dish before serving.

FRUIT PUNCH

SERVES: 6

600 ml (1 pint) diluted Ribena
300 ml (½ pint) apple juice
1 cinnamon stick
1 apple, quartered, cored and chopped

PREPARATION: 2 minutes
COOKING: 5 minutes

1. Put Ribena and apple juice into a saucepan.
2. Break cinnamon stick into large pieces. Add apple and cinnamon to the Ribena mixture.
3. Bring slowly to simmering point them remove from heat and allow to cool slightly. Discard cinnamon and ladle drink into plastic beakers. Check temperature before serving to children.

DEVILLED CHICKEN WINGS

MAKES: 12

12 chicken wings
2 tbsp apricot jam
2 tbsp oil
1 tbsp vinegar
¼ tsp chilli powder
¼ tsp turmeric
salt and freshly ground black pepper

PREPARATION: 5 minutes
COOKING: 40 minutes

1. Preheat the oven to 220°C, 425°F, Gas 7. Arrange

chicken wings in a single layer in a roasting tin.

2. Mix remaining ingredients together and brush over the chicken. Roast for 35-40 minutes, turning once or twice and brushing with apricot mixture. Cook until golden brown and juices run clear when a skewer is inserted into the flesh.

3. Arrange in a large dish and leave to cool before serving.

SAUSAGE ROLLS

MAKES: 42

1 leek or small onion, finely chopped
450 g (1 lb) sausagemeat
75 g (3 oz) sweetcorn, thawed if frozen
salt and freshly ground black pepper
500 g (1 lb 2 oz) packet puff pastry, thawed if frozen
1 egg, beaten

PREPARATION: 30 minutes
COOKING: 15 minutes

1. Preheat the oven to 220°C, 425°F, Gas 7. Mix leek or onion together with the sausagemeat, sweetcorn and seasoning (use a food

Above: Sausage Rolls
Below: Devilled Chicken Wings

processor if you have one). Divide mixture into four.

2. On a lightly floured surface, roll out half the pastry to form a rectangle measuring 23 x 30 cm (9 x 12 inches). Cut in half lengthways to make two 11.5 cm (4½ inch) wide strips.

3. Take one portion of sausagemeat and place in strip along one side of a piece of pastry. Repeat with second portion of sausagemeat and pastry.

4. Brush a little egg along the edge of the pastry. Fold the pastry over the filling and press edges to seal. Cut into thick slices, place on a baking sheet sprinkled with water.

5. Repeat steps 2, 3 and 4 with remaining pastry and sausagemeat.

6. Brush the tops of the sausage rolls with egg, and cook for 15 minutes until the pastry is golden brown. Leave to cool.

MAGIC TOADSTOOLS

MAKES: 6

6 hard-boiled eggs, shelled
6 slices processed cheese
2 tbsp mayonnaise
3 tomatoes, halved
To decorate:
mustard and cress

PREPARATION: 10 minutes

1. Trim the top and bottom off each hard-boiled egg and arrange them slightly apart on a serving plate.
2. Cut out circles from the slices of cheese with a 6.5 cm (2½ inch) plain pastry cutter.

Stick on top of each egg using a little mayonnaise to secure firmly in place.

3. Place tomatoes cut side down on to cheese, again using a little mayonnaise to secure in place.
4. Spoon the remaining mayonnaise into a greaseproof paper piping bag. Snip off tip of piping bag and pipe small dots over the top of the tomatoes.

Decorate plate with mustard and cress to resemble grass.

Below: Magic Toadstools

BISCUIT BEARS

MAKES: 12

225 g (8 oz) plain flour
50 g (2 oz) caster sugar
125 g (5 oz) butter
grated rind of 1 small orange
1 tbsp orange juice
To decorate:
125 g (5 oz) ready-to-roll
** icing**
red or pink paste colouring
12 glacé cherries, halved
24 chocolate dots

PREPARATION: 25 minutes
COOKING: 10 minutes

1. Preheat the oven to 180°C, 350°F, Gas 4. Put the flour

and caster sugar into a bowl.
Cut the butter into small
pieces, then rub into the flour
until the mixture resembles
fine crumbs.

2. Stir in the orange rind and
juice, then mould the mixture
into a ball with your hands.

3. On a floured surface, knead
the dough lightly. Roll out
until 5 mm (¼ inch) thick,
then stamp out twelve 7.5 cm
(3 inch) circles with a plain
cutter. Reserve trimmings to
make bears' ears.

4. Arrange the circles slightly
apart on two baking sheets.
Reknead remaining dough and
roll out. Cut out small circles
and halve, then arrange on the
biscuits as ears.

5. Cook the biscuits for
10 minutes until a pale golden
colour. Carefully loosen with a
palette knife and set biscuits
aside to cool.

6. Shape half of the icing into
small circles for the eyes and
stick on to the biscuits with a
little water.

7. Colour the remaining icing
pink. Roll out on a surface
dusted with icing sugar and
stamp out twelve 4 cm
(1½ inch) circles for snouts.
Stick on to biscuits with a
little water.

8. Add the halved glacé
cherries for the bears' noses,
slices of glacé cherry halves for
their mouths and chocolate
dots for their eyes. Press into
the icing to secure.

CHOCOLATE KRISPIES

MAKES: 56

**150 g (6 oz) cooking
   chocolate**
2 tbsp golden syrup
**50 g (2oz) butter or
   margarine**
100 g (4 oz) Rice Krispies

PREPARATION: 3 minutes
(plus 1-2 hours chilling)
COOKING: 2-3 minutes

1. Break chocolate into
a saucepan, add the
syrup and butter or
margarine and heat
gently for 2-3 min-
utes until melted.

2. Carefully stir in the
Rice Krispies until they
are evenly coated with

Above: Biscuit Bears
Below: Chocolate Krispies

melted chocolate.

3. Separate some petit four
cases and fill with teaspoonfuls
of the Krispie mixture. Chill
for 1-2 hours until set.

4. Krispies may be stored in
airtight box for up to 5 days.

C·H·I·L·D·R·E·N'S P·A·R·T·I·E·S

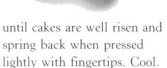

LITTLE LADYBIRDS

MAKES: 24

Cake:
150 g (6 oz) self-raising flour
150 g (6 oz) caster sugar
150 g (6 oz) soft margarine
3 eggs
Butter icing:
225 g (8 oz) butter, softened
450 g (1 lb) icing sugar,
* sifted*
red paste food colouring
To decorate:
red and black sweets from a
* 115 g (4½ oz) packet milk*
* chocolate M&M's*
100 g (4 oz) packet milk
* chocolate Minstrels*
piece of angelica

PREPARATION: 35 minutes
COOKING: 15-20 minutes

1. Preheat the oven to 180°C, 350°F, Gas 4. Mix all the cake ingredients together in a bowl until completely smooth.
2. Place 24 paper cake cases in the moulds of two bun trays. Divide mixture between cases.
3. Cook for 15-20 minutes

until cakes are well risen and spring back when pressed lightly with fingertips. Cool.
4. Beat the icing ingredients together until mixture is light and fluffy.
5. Peel off cases and place cakes upside down on a tray. Cover with icing. Add M&M's for spots, whole Minstrels for heads, halved ones for feet and angelica for eyes and antennae.

BANANA & HONEY CAKES

MAKES: 10

1 small banana
50 g (2 oz) sunflower
* margarine*
25 g (1 oz) caster sugar
25 g (1 oz) clear honey
75 g (3 oz) self-raising flour
1 egg
To decorate:
25 g (1 oz) sunflower
* margarine*
50 g (2 oz) icing sugar
10 sugar flowers

PREPARATION: 15 minutes
COOKING: 12 minutes

Above: Little Ladybirds
Right: Banana & Honey Cakes

1. Preheat the oven to 180°C, 350°F, Gas 4. Line ten sections of a tartlet tray with paper cases.
2. Put all the cake ingredients into a food processor and mix together until smooth. Alternatively, mash the banana, then beat together with the remaining cake ingredients.
3. Spoon mixture into paper cases and cook for 12 minutes until well risen and golden brown. Leave to cool.
4. To decorate, beat margarine and icing sugar together. Spoon a little on to each cake and top with a sugar flower.

P·R·A·C·T·I·C·A·L·I·T·I·E·S

- Oven temperatures vary: keep an eye on cakes while cooking.
- Paste food colourings are more intense than liquid ones, so use slightly less.
- Store cakes in an airtight tin for up to three days. Freeze for up to one month.

C·H·I·L·D·R·E·N'·S P·A·R·T·I·E·S

TOFFEE APPLES

MAKES: 8

8 small dessert apples
8 small wooden skewers
4 tbsp golden syrup
325 g (12 oz) granulated
   sugar
25 g (1 oz) butter
1 tsp white wine vinegar
4 tbsp water

PREPARATION: 5 minutes
COOKING: 8 minutes

1. Wash and dry apples and push a wooden skewer through the core of each.
2. Place the remaining ingredients in a large saucepan and heat gently, without stirring, until all of the sugar has completely dissolved.
3. Bring to the boil and boil rapidly for about 6-8 minutes until the mixture changes colour to deep brown. Use a sugar thermometer to check if the toffee is ready: it should read 143°C, 290°F. If you don't have a thermometer, remove the pan from the heat and drop a teaspoonful of toffee into a glass of cold water. If the toffee snaps cleanly when removed from the water it is ready.
4. Remove the pan from the heat, dip each apple into the toffee and swirl to coat evenly. Stand the apples on a lightly oiled baking sheet and leave aside to cool.
5. Wrap in squares of cellophane and tie with ribbon. Store for up to 3 days in a cool, dry place.

Above: Toffee Apples
Below: Creeping Caterpillar

CHOCOLATE HEDGEHOGS

MAKES: 24

Cake:
125 g (5 oz) self-raising flour
25 g (1 oz) cocoa powder
150 g (6 oz) caster sugar
150 g (6 oz) soft margarine
3 eggs
Butter icing:
150 g (6 oz) butter, softened
325 g (12 oz) icing sugar, sifted
25 g (1 oz) cocoa power, sifted
To decorate:
5 chocolate flakes
115 g (4½ oz) packet milk chocolate M&M's
mini bag Jelly Tots

PREPARATION: 45 minutes
COOKING: 15-20 minutes

1. Make cakes as in steps 1, 2 and 3 of Little Ladybirds (see page 96).
2. Beat icing ingredients together. Spread over cakes.
3. Split chocolate flakes and stick into cakes to resemble spines. Add M&M's for eyes and Jelly Tots for noses.

Above: Chocolate Hedgehogs

CREEPING CATERPILLARS

MAKES: 7

Cake:
100 g (4 oz) self-raising flour
100 g (4 oz) caster sugar
100 g (4 oz) soft margarine
2 eggs
Icing:
225 g (8 oz) icing sugar, sifted
about 2 tbsp water
green food colouring
To decorate:
14 round Dolly Mixtures
2 glacé cherries
piece of angelica
2 tbsp sugar strands

PREPARATION: 30 minutes
COOKING: 10-15 minutes

1. Preheat the oven to 180°C, 350°F, Gas 4. Mix all the cake ingredients in a bowl until smooth.
2. Place 42 petit four cases on a baking sheet. Divide mixture between cases.
3. Cook for 10-15 minutes until cakes are well risen and spring back when pressed lightly with fingertips. Cool.
4. To make icing, mix icing sugar with water to form consistency of pouring custard. Stir in a few drops of food colouring.
5. Add a little icing to top of each cake. Make seven faces by adding Dolly Mixtures for eyes, slice of cherry for mouth and angelica for antennae. Sprinkle sugar strands over remaining cakes. Leave to set.
6. Arrange one face cake with five plain cakes for body.

· C H A P T E R 8 ·

P·A·R·T·Y
C·A·K·E·S

This selection of stunning party cakes will enable you to make your child's dream come true and give her the best birthday cake she's ever seen. Any one of these fabulous cakes will be the perfect showpiece for the party table. Don't forget the candles for the perfect finishing touch!

CAT CAKE

SERVES: 8

Cake:

150 g (6 oz) soft margarine
150 g (6 oz) caster sugar
3 eggs, beaten
150 g (6 oz) self-raising flour
50 g (2 oz) plain flour
25 g (1 oz) cocoa powder
1 tbsp milk

To decorate:

cornflour, for dusting
2 x 250 g (9 oz) packets ready-to-roll icing
little honey or jam
200 g (7 oz) icing sugar
25 g (1 oz) cocoa powder
100 g (4 oz) butter, softened
1 Swiss roll
brown, green and black paste food colouring
½ x 75 g (3 oz) packet choco-late wafer stick biscuits
6 chocolate sticks

PREPARATION: 15 minutes
COOKING: 1½ hours
(plus 1 hour to assemble)

1. Preheat the oven to 160°C, 325°F, Gas 3. Grease and line the base of a 1.1 litre (2 pint) pudding basin.
2. To make the cake, beat the margarine and sugar together until light and fluffy. Gradually add the eggs, alternating with the flours, to margarine mixture. Sift the cocoa powder and stir in with the milk, beat until smooth.
3. Spoon into basin and level top. Cook for 1½ hours or until well risen. To test, insert a skewer into centre of cake: it should come out clean.
4. Leave cake to cool slightly then loosen edge and turn out on to a cooling rack. Leave to cool completely.

5. On a surface dusted with a little cornflour, roll out one-third of the icing until large enough to cover a 28 cm (11 inch) cake board.
6. Spread edges of board with a little honey or jam, lift icing over a rolling pin, position on board and smooth with fingertips. Trim edges.
7. To make butter icing, sift icing sugar and cocoa together then gradually beat into butter until smooth.
8. Cut cake in half vertically. Place one half, cut side down, on to cake board to make the cat's body, leaving space for the Swiss roll 'broomstick' to go underneath. Trim remaining half of cake into a rounded shape for the cat's head and position on the board cut side down.
9. Spread the butter icing over the cat, covering it completely. Reserve remainder.
10. Trim ends of Swiss roll slightly and cut a slice off lengthways to give a flat edge. Set aside this slice of Swiss roll to make cat's tail. Colour half of remaining ready-to-roll icing brown, roll out and use to cover Swiss roll.
11. Trim and place under cat to resemble broomstick. Add chocolate wafer biscuits to one end to look like twigs and secure in place with a little of the reserved butter icing.
12. Cut a tail shape from remaining Swiss roll, place

over broomstick and cover with reserved butter icing.

13. Add chocolate sticks to make cat's whiskers. Colour a little of the remaining ready-to-roll icing green and shape to resemble eyes. Put in place. Colour some of the icing brown to make a triangle nose and ears. Attach the cat's nose to the whiskers using a little butter icing.

14. Colour remaining ready-to-roll icing black and make a pointed hat, then add to the cat with the ears.

15. Store in a cool place until ready to serve.

P·R·A·C·T·I·C·A·L·I·T·I·E·S

• Our Cat Cake makes a delightful centrepiece for a Hallowe'en party. Serve with Crispy Snails (page 88), Potato Skins & Avocado Dip, Devilled Chicken Wings, Fruit Punch (page 92) and Toffee Apples (page 98).

FOUR-WHEEL DRIVE

SERVES: 20

a little oil
Cake:
325 g (12 oz) soft margarine
325 g (12 oz) caster sugar
325 g (12 oz) self-raising flour
150 g (6 oz) plain flour
6 eggs, beaten
2 oranges, grated rind and
*   2 tbsp juice*
30 x 20 cm (12 x 18 inch)
*   cake board*
Butter icing:
100 g (4 oz) butter, softened
1 tbsp orange juice
225 g (8 oz) icing sugar,
*   sifted*
black, green and blue paste
*   food colourings*
3 tbsp apricot jam
500 g (1 lb 2 oz) packet white
*   marzipan*
cornflour, for dusting
2 x 500 g (1 lb 2 oz) packets
*   ready-to-roll fondant icing*
8 liquorice Catherine wheels
1 egg white
100 g (4 oz) foil-wrapped
*   toffees*
4 candles and candleholders

PREPARATION: 30 minutes (plus
2½ hours decorating time)
COOKING: 1½ hours

1. Preheat the oven to 160°C,
325°F, Gas 3. Brush base and
sides of a 900 g (2 lb) loaf tin
and a 28 x 18 x 4 cm (11 x 7 x
1½ inch) roasting tin with a
little oil. Line base of both tins
with greaseproof paper and
brush with oil.
2. To make sponge cake, put
margarine and sugar in a bowl
and beat until light. Gradually
beat in the flours and eggs a
little at a time until smooth.
Beat in orange rind and juice.
Half fill the loaf tin and spoon
the remaining mixture into
roasting tin. Level the surfaces.
3. Cook cake in roasting tin for
about 1¼ hours and loaf tin
cake for about 1½ hours. Swop
shelf position of cakes halfway
through. To test: cakes should
be well risen and a skewer
should come out cleanly when
inserted into the centre.
4. Cool slightly, then turn out
cakes on to a cooling rack.
Remove tins and paper and
leave to cool completely.
5. Place roasting tin cake on a
chopping board. Place bottom
of loaf tin cake on top of large
cake so that loaf cake is right
in one corner of roasting tin
cake. Cut large cake out
around side of loaf tin cake
and 7.5 cm (3 inches) beyond
the end to form the base of the
driver's cab.
6. Place two cakes in position
on cake board. Cut remaining
cake into two strips widthways
and stand on top of base cake
to form driver's cab.
7. To make the butter icing,
cut the butter into pieces and
put in a large bowl with the
orange juice and half the icing
sugar. Beat together until the
mixture is light and fluffy.
Gradually beat in remaining
icing sugar and mix well.
8. Sandwich cakes together with
butter icing. Colour remainder
grey using a little black food
colouring and spread around
sides of base cake.
9. Warm the apricot jam, sieve
and brush over top and sides
of the un-iced cake.
10. Knead the marzipan, roll
out thinly on a surface lightly
dusted with cornflour. Cut
strips and use to cover areas
brushed with apricot jam.
11. Colour one packet of

fondant icing green. Colour two-thirds of the other packet of fondant icing blue, half of the remaining fondant icing grey and leave the rest white. Wrap each icing portion tightly in separate plastic bags so that it doesn't dry out.

12. Brush a little jam on marzipan sides of lorry. Roll out one-third of the green fondant icing on a surface dusted with cornflour and use to cover one side of the lorry. Smooth with fingertips dusted with cornflour. Fold top edge over to form a ridge and trim bottom edges so that they overhang butter icing slightly.

13. Knead trimmings with half remaining green icing and repeat to cover other side of lorry. Cover back and front edge of lorry in the same way.

14. Brush driver's cab with jam. Roll out portions of blue fondant icing and cover cab.

15. Press four liquorice Catherine wheels into butter icing on each side of the lorry.

Brush above wheels with some of the egg white. Shape ropes of blue fondant icing and press above wheels to resemble the lorry's mudguards.

16. Roll out white fondant icing and cut windows for the driver's cab. Stick in place with a little egg white. Cut out two number fours and stick on each side of the lorry with egg white. Then add a green door and a white handle on each side of the cake.

17. Roll out a little grey fondant icing and cut radiator grill. Stick on to front of cab with egg white. Shape bumper from rope of grey fondant and stick in place with egg white.

18. Wipe cake board. Leave to dry overnight.

19. Arrange sweets on the top of the lorry and press candles in candleholders into the roof of the driver's cab.

DOG CAKE

SERVES: 16

*12.5 cm (5 inch) round cake
    (see Basic Cake Recipe,
    opposite)*
*2 x 18 cm (7 inch) sandwich
    cakes (see Basic Cake
    Recipe, opposite)*
Filling:
225 g (8 oz) butter, softened
*450 g (1 lb) icing sugar,
    sifted*
To decorate:
*25 x 35.5 cm (10 x 14 inch)
    cake board*
*675 g (1½ lb) ready-to-roll
    fondant icing*
cornflour, for dusting
4 tbsp cocoa powder, sifted
*black, red, blue and brown
    paste food colourings*
3 icing flowers

DECORATING: 1¼ hours

1. Trim top of small cake to
make it level, if necessary. Cut
a small curve from both of the
sandwich cakes so they each
fit snugly to smaller cake.
Split the small cake in half
horizontally.
2. Beat filling ingredients
together until fluffy. Spread a
little over edges of cake board.
3. Knead and roll out 450 g
(1 lb) fondant on a surface
lightly dusted with cornflour.
Use to cover the cake board.
Smooth surface and trim away
excess. Reserve the trimmings
tightly wrapped in clingfilm.
4. Spoon half the butter icing

BASIC CAKE RECIPE

To make:	12.5 cm (5 inch)	2 x 18 cm (7 inch)	18 cm (7 inch)	23 cm (9 inch)
Cake tins	round	sandwich	square	round
Eggs	2	3	4	5
Soft margarine	100 g (4 oz)	175 g (6 oz)	225 g (8 oz)	275 g (10 oz)
Caster sugar	100 g (4 oz)	175 g (6 oz)	225 g (8 oz)	275 g (10 oz)
Self-raising flour	100 g (4 oz)	175 g (6 oz)	225 g (8 oz)	275 g (10 oz)
Plain flour	50 g (2 oz)	75 g (3 oz)	100 g (4 oz)	125 g (5 oz)
Milk	2 tsp	3 tsp	4 tsp	5 tsp
Cooking time	35 minutes	20-25 minutes	1 hour	1 hour 10 mins

1. Preheat the oven to 180°C, 350°F, Gas 4, for sandwich cakes, and 160°C, 325°F, Gas 3, for other cakes.
2. Lightly oil all cake tins. Line base of sandwich tins with greaseproof paper. Line base and sides of other tins. Brush lightly with oil.
3. Measure ingredients, using the chart above as a guide.

Place all ingredients in a bowl and beat with electric whisk or wooden spoon until just mixed. Spoon into prepared tins and level surfaces.
4. Place in the oven and cook for the times shown in the chart until the cakes are well risen and golden brown. To test: sandwich cakes should spring back when pressed with

fingertips. For other cakes, a skewer should come out clean when inserted into the centre of the cakes.
5. Loosen edges, turn cake out on to a clean wire rack. Peel away the paper from the bottom of sponge. Put the sponge to one side to cool. Trim the top level if it looks uneven.

into a second bowl and beat in cocoa. Use plain butter icing to sandwich cakes together and arrange on the cake board to resemble a head and body. Spread top and sides thinly with the remaining plain butter icing as a base coat.
5. Cover the top and sides of the cake with brown butter icing and rough up the surface of cake with a knife.
6. Shape eyes and a mouth from white fondant trimmings.

Left: Dog Cake

Press on to cake. Colour a little fondant black and a little red. Shape nose and eyeballs from black and a tongue from red fondant icing. Stick on to cake with a little butter icing.
7. Colour half the remaining fondant pale blue and the remainder brown. Roll out blue and cut a waistcoat, stick on to cake and decorate with icing flowers for the buttons. Roll out brown icing and cut ears and paws, and then stick them on to cake. Store the cake in a cool place until ready to serve.

P·R·A·C·T·I·C·A·L·I·T·I·E·S

- If you don't want to buy a cake board, cover a tray or chopping board with silver foil instead.
- Pop a piece of cake into each child's take-home party bag – the children may be too full to eat the cake at the party.
- Serve diluted fresh fruit juice in plastic cups with lids and holes in the top for straws to prevent spills.
- A pack of wipes is useful for cleaning sticky hands and faces after the children have finished eating.
- A pvc tablecloth will save your table from damage and is wonderfully easy to clean.

ELEPHANT CAKE

SERVES: 20

18 cm (7 inch) square cake
  (see Basic Cake Recipe,
  page 105)
2 x 18 cm (7 inch) sandwich
  cakes (see Basic Cake
  Recipe, page 105)
Filling:
175 g (6 oz) butter, softened
325 g (12 oz) icing sugar,
  sifted
To decorate:
25 x 35.5 cm (10 x 14 inch)
  cake board
1.4 kg (3 lb) ready-to-roll
  fondant icing
cornflour, for dusting
red and black paste food
  colourings
little egg white

DECORATING: 1½ hours

1. Place square cake on a chopping board. Cut one sandwich cake in half to make two semicircles, place on top of each other then butt straight edge of semicircles against top left corner of square cake.
2. Put second sandwich cake on top of semicircles so that it overlaps square cake to make elephant's head. Curve top right-hand corner for elephant's bottom and cut legs. Split square cake in half horizontally.
3. Beat filling ingredients together until fluffy. Spread a

little over edges of cake board.
4. Knead and roll out 450 g (1 lb) fondant icing on a surface dusted with cornflour. Use to cover cake board. Smooth surface and trim. Reserve trimmings wrapped in clingfilm.
5. Sandwich cakes together with two-thirds of the remaining filling, and arrange on cake board to resemble head and body. Reserve 2 tsp of filling and spread remainder thinly over top and sides of the cake.
6. Knead fondant icing (not trimmings) and colour red. Roll out on a surface dusted with cornflour until a little larger than top and sides of cake. Lift icing over rolling pin, drape over the cake and smooth with fingertips dipped in cornflour.

Above: Elephant Cake

7. Trim away any excess icing. Brush away cornflour with a dry pastry brush. Shape ears and trunk from red fondant trimmings. Place ears on two pieces of card for support, position on cake and stick in place with reserved filling. Support the end of the elephant's trunk using a small ball of the red fondant icing.
8. Roll out half of the white fondant trimmings and cut three circles using a small pastry cutter; halve and stick on to elephant's feet with egg white to make toenails. Shape two eyes, tusks and an oval shape to fit into the end of the trunk. Stick them in place with egg white.
9. Colour the remaining white fondant trimmings black, and

shape two eyeballs. Stick them in place using a little egg white. Leave the icing to dry for several hours or, alternatively, leave overnight.

TEATIME EXPRESS

MAKES: 1 train

Cake:
85 g (3½ oz) self-raising flour
15 g (½ oz) cocoa powder
¼ tsp baking powder
100 g (4 oz) caster sugar
100 g (4 oz) soft margarine
2 eggs
4 tbsp apricot jam, warmed
Icing:
50 g (2 oz) soft margarine
50 g (2 oz) cocoa powder
325 g (12 oz) icing sugar, sifted
3-4 tbsp milk
To decorate:
250 g (9 oz) Liquorice Allsorts
mini bag Jelly Tots
50 g (2 oz) Dolly Mixtures
50 g (2 oz) Jelly Bears
2 red liquorice bootlaces

PREPARATION: 40 minutes
COOKING: 20-25 minutes

1. Preheat the oven to 180°C, 350°F, Gas 4. Mix all the cake ingredients, except jam, together in a bowl until completely smooth.
2. Grease and line the base of an 18 cm (7 inch) square tin. Spoon in the mixture and level the surface.
3. Cook for 20-25 minutes until cake is well risen and springs back when pressed lightly with fingertips.
4. Turn cake out on to a cooling rack and remove paper. When cool, cut into six bars. Halve one and place one half over a second bar to make the engine. Use three bars for trucks, cut remaining 1½ bars into eight strips. Using jam, stick two strips under the engine, one at each end, to form 'axles' for the wheels. Do the same for each truck.
5. To make icing, melt margarine in a saucepan. Sift the cocoa powder and stir in

Below: Teatime Express

to the margarine. Cook for 1 minute. Take off heat and stir in icing sugar and milk. Beat until the icing is the consistency of pouring custard. Stir in more milk if needed.
6. Spread top and sides of cakes thinly with jam. Stand on a rack over a baking sheet.
7. Spoon icing over to cover cakes completely and smooth with a knife dipped in hot water. Reheat icing if it thickens.
8. Leave for 1 to 2 minutes, then add Liquorice Allsorts for wheels, funnel and windows. Fill trucks with assorted sweets.
9. Arrange the liquorice bootlaces on a large plate to make a track, and place the train on top.

P·R·A·C·T·I·C·A·L·I·T·I·E·S

• If you've spent ages making a cake don't forget to take a picture of it before it's demolished. Your child will enjoy looking back at it and you'll have a record of your brilliant baking!

RABBIT CAKE

SERVES: 24

*23 cm (9 inch) round cake
    (see Basic Cake Recipe,
    page 105)*
*2 x 18 cm (7 inch) sandwich
    cakes (see Basic Cake
    Recipe, page 105)*
Filling:
350 g (12 oz) butter, softened
*675 g (1½ lb) icing sugar,
    sifted*
To decorate:
*30 x 40 cm (12 x 16 inch)
    cake board*
*675 g (1½ lb) ready-to-roll
    fondant icing*
*green, pink or red and black
    paste food colourings*
2 plain mini Swiss rolls

DECORATING: 1½ hours

1. Trim top of large cake, if necessary, and place on a chopping board. Hold one sandwich cake slightly overlapping the top of the larger cake. Using it as a guide, cut a crescent shape out of larger cake and remove. Reserve cake trimmings.
2. Split large round cake in half horizontally.
3. Cut the cake trimming in half. Cut one half into two for feet, and cut remaining piece into a tail shape.
4. Beat the filling ingredients together until fluffy. Spread a little over edges of cake board.
5. Knead and roll out 450 g (1 lb) fondant icing on surface

dusted with cornflour. Use to cover cake board. Smooth surface and trim. Reserve trimmings, wrapped in clingfilm.
6. Spoon half the butter icing into a second bowl and colour pale green. Use plain butter icing to sandwich cakes together. Arrange on cake board so that cakes fit snugly together and resemble head

and body. Add mini Swiss rolls for ears. Spread tail thickly with butter icing and spread a very thin layer over top and sides of all remaining cakes as a base coat.
7. Spread green butter icing thickly over top and sides of cakes, excluding tail, and rough up with a knife.
8. Colour white fondant (not trimmings) pink, and shape

CLOCK CAKE

SERVES: 8

Cake:
150 g (6 oz) self-raising flour
½ tsp baking powder
150 g (6 oz) caster sugar
150 g (6 oz) soft margarine
3 eggs
grated rind of 1 lemon
Butter icing:
150 g (6 oz) butter, softened
325 g (12 oz) icing sugar,
* sifted*
1 tbsp lemon juice
To decorate:
150 g (6 oz) ready-to-roll
* icing*
red, blue and yellow paste
* food colourings*
number cutters

PREPARATION: 35 minutes
COOKING: 20-25 minutes

1. Preheat the oven to 180°C, 350°F, Gas 4. Mix all the cake ingredients together in a bowl until completely smooth.
2. Grease and line the base of two 18 cm (7 inch) sandwich tins. Divide mixture between the two tins and level surfaces.
3. Cook for 20-25 minutes until cakes are well risen and spring back when pressed with fingertips.
4. Turn cakes out on to a cooling rack and remove paper. Leave to cool.
5. Beat the butter icing ingredients together until light and fluffy. Spread half of the butter icing on top of one cake and sandwich the cakes together. Place on a serving plate and spread the remaining icing over the top of the cake.
6. Divide the ready-to-roll icing into three and colour one piece red, one blue and one yellow. Roll out the red and blue icing on a surface dusted with cornflour. Stamp out the numbers with cutters and position on the cake.
7. Shape the clock hands from the yellow icing and press on to the cake.

cheeks and nose, press on to cake. Roll out remainder and cut shapes for inside ears, then press on to cake.
9. Shape the rabbit's teeth, whiskers and eyes from the white fondant trimmings. Colour a little fondant black, and shape the eyeballs, then stick them on to the cake. Keep in a cool place until you are ready to serve.

Above left:
Rabbit Cake
Right: Clock Cake

THE BIG TOP

SERVES: 26

a little oil
Cake:
225 g (8 oz) soft margarine
225 g (8 oz) caster sugar
225 g (8 oz) self-raising flour
100 g (4 oz) plain flour
4 eggs, beaten
grated rind of 1 orange
4 tsp orange juice
To decorate:
28 x 25 cm (11 x 10 inch)
*   cake board*
2 tbsp apricot jam
2 x 500 g (1 lb 2 oz) packets
*   ready-to-roll fondant icing*
cornflour, for dusting
red, black, brown, blue,
*   yellow, green paste food*
*   colourings*
egg white
50 g (2 oz) icing sugar, sifted
3 candles and candleholders

PREPARATION: 25 minutes
(plus 3 hours decorating time)
COOKING: 1¼ hours

1. Preheat the oven to 160°C, 325°F, Gas 3. Brush base and sides of a 28 x 18 x 4 cm (11 x 7 x 1½ inch) roasting tin with oil. Line base and sides of tin with a large piece of greaseproof paper and snip into corners so paper fits snugly up the sides. Brush with oil.
2. To make sponge cake, put margarine and caster sugar in a bowl and beat until light and fluffy. Gradually beat in the

flours and eggs a little at a time until mixture is smooth. Beat in orange rind and juice and spoon into prepared tin. Level surface and then cook for about 1¼ hours. To test: the cake should be well risen and a skewer should come out cleanly when it is inserted into the centre of the cake.
3. Cool slightly, then turn out the cake on to a cooling rack. Remove tin and paper and leave to cool
4. Cut away the two corners from top of cake to resemble circus roof. Put cake on cake board. Warm apricot jam, sieve out lumps and brush over the top and sides of cake.
5. Roll out half of one packet of fondant icing and use to cover the main square of cake. Smooth with fingertips dipped in cornflour. Trim the excess and reserve, tightly wrapped in a plastic bag so that it doesn't dry out.
6. Roll out the remaining half of opened packet of fondant icing and use to cover roof top and roof sides of big top. Trim and keep excess as before.
7. Roll out half of the second packet of fondant to a rectangle about 20 x 15 cm (8 x 6 inches). Trim edges neatly and position on one half of the cake, closely butting up to roof, to resemble one side of big top opening. Peel back bottom centre corner over top

of cake. Smooth fondant icing over cake top and sides with fingertips dipped in a little cornflour. Trim excess and keep as before.
8. Repeat to make second side of big top. Wipe board.
9. Knead all trimmings and the remaining fondant icing together. Reserve a tiny piece for clown's ruff and wrap in clingfilm. Colour one-quarter of the icing red. Wrap tightly in a plastic bag.
10. Shape four small balls from the fondant icing, colour one pink, one grey, one brown and the last one blue. Divide remaining icing in half and colour one half yellow and the other green. Wrap all colours separately in clingfilm.
11. Roll out half the red icing thinly and cut thin strips for the stripes on the big top. Arrange on big top, sticking in place with a little egg white. Continue using more red fondant icing until both sides of the big top are completed.
12. From red coloured icing cut out a flag shape and a small banner shape for child's name. Stick banner on to cake with egg white. Leave flag to dry on cake board.
13. Roll out a little of the green fondant icing, cut tiny triangles and arrange on top of red strips along the base of the roof. Stick in place with egg white. Cut a thin strip of yellow with a pastry wheel,

and position just above the green bunting.

14. Decorate the opening of the big top with animals and performers cut from the reserved coloured icing, rolled out and cut with a small knife. Make the lion's mane by pressing a little icing through a fine sieve.

15. Leave the cake to dry overnight then using food colouring, paint on the animals' features. Mix icing sugar with a few drops of water or the remaining egg white and use to pipe the child's name on to the banner (or use ready-made icing letters). Stick the flag in place with icing and pipe on the child's age.

16. Position three candles in candleholders on the cake.

111